the Battle

The Battle of the
Komandorski Islands

JOHN A. LORELLI

The Battle of the Komandorski Islands, March 1943

NAVAL INSTITUTE PRESS
Annapolis, Maryland

Library of Congress Cataloging in Publication Data
Lorelli, John A., 1946–
The battle of the Komandorski Islands, March 1943.
Bibliography: p.
Includes index.
1. Commander Islands (R.S.F.S.R.), Battle of, 1943.
I. Title.
D764.3.C66L67   1984   940.54′26   84-975
ISBN 0-87021-093-9

Printed in the United States of America

To
Lloyd Ames Berg 1947–1974,
who was my shipmate and friend,
and to
Anthony John Lorelli,
who is my son

Contents

Preface

This story has been a long time in the making. I became interested in it when I was twelve years old, having just read Samuel Eliot Morison's account of the battle. The image of slim-hulled destroyers charging a powerful enemy force never really left me. When the time came to decide army, air force, or navy, there was no hesitation. Destroyers had changed a lot between 1943 and 1967, but a story read years before had helped make me a destroyer sailor and thereby forever solidified my interest in naval matters. Entertaining a whim, I got the official records of the battle from the naval archives in 1972. Unfortunately, it was not until 1981 that I was able to set out in pursuit of my story.

To say that I was amazed and then delighted by the cooperation I received in writing about a battle that happened over forty years ago would be an understatement. The aid I have received at every turn will be repaid, I hope, by the effort and care I have tried to put into the retelling of the story. I have tried to write this account in a way that will not only be technically correct, but will portray the mood of the times, the life in the ships, and the feelings of the men involved. It is also my hope that this story will stand as a record of gallant men who served their country well.

I would be more than remiss if I did not specifically thank several people. They are: John Atkeson, Worthy Bitler, Jim Brewer, Vince Dahlen, Father Richard Hodge, Bill Hosey, Jerry Miller, George O'Connell, Al Ovrum, Ken Robinson, Paul Stillwell, Chuck Vasey, Mary Anderson, W. H. Hutchinson, and MaryJane O'Hagan. I am especially grateful to Captain J. F. B. Johnston, USN (Ret.). Ben Johnston has been unstinting in his support. He has spent countless hours giving me a feel for the prewar navy, patiently explaining the intricacies of trying to hit the other fellow's ship across ten miles of seascape, telling me who to contact, and rooting more than a few names from the Naval Academy Register. He has also made phone calls, written letters on my behalf, and done his best to correct my poor usage of naval terminology. In short, he has given me a standard of excellence I have tried hard to meet. He has been the kind of friend we all wish we had or wish we could be. I am in his debt.

I also owe thanks to the archivists of the Operational Archives Branch and to Little, Brown & Company for permission to quote from *The Two-Ocean War*. Finally, I am indebted to Carol Swartz of the Naval Institute Press. Everyone who thinks he can write is sure every word is perfectly chosen. It is the sometimes unenviable lot of an editor to set matters straight. I like what Carol has done.

To all who took the time to answer my letters and questions, but who are not mentioned in the text, I offer my gratitude. As much as I tried to weave everyone's account into the narrative, it simply wasn't possible. The same goes for the many mentions made of men who were well-known personalities to their shipmates, but who do not appear here; some have died in the intervening years or simply chose not to contribute. No man should feel offended if he isn't mentioned. Everyone contributed something to this story.

Whatever error in timing or the sequence of events there

might be in this narrative is solely my fault. I have tried to be meticulous in getting it right, but in sorting out contradictory memories and contradictory records, the chance for error remains. I have exercised my prerogative to convert the West Longitude dates and times found in Japanese records to the East Longitude dates and times found in American records. Any error of computation is mine. Naval rank given with individual names is as of 26 March 1943.

Writing this story has been a rewarding experience. I have always considered myself a navy man, so it has been a distinct pleasure to have spent so much time corresponding with, and in the company of, so many top-notch navy men.

JOHN A. LORELLI

Introduction

"Close your hearts to pity." With those words, Adolf Hitler sent his army slashing into Poland on 1 September 1939. Six years and one day later, on the deck of an American battleship anchored in Tokyo Bay, World War II came to an end. The Japanese surrender delegation affixed their names to the document of surrender and stood stiffly at attention as General of the Army Douglas MacArthur fittingly intoned, "These proceedings are closed." For just a moment, a world convulsed by 2,194 days of global slaughter paused to catch its breath and count its millions of dead. The world of September 1945 was indeed "The World Turned Upside Down."[1] The armored division, the long-range bomber, the aircraft carrier, the atomic bomb, total war, had brought mankind to the brink of Armageddon. Thoughtful men the world over decreed that such a thing must never happen again. Though countless civil, anticolonial, and regional wars have occurred since World War II, mankind has never again plunged into the abyss of world war.

1

INTRODUCTION

Nearly four decades have passed since that dimly remembered day in Tokyo Bay. All the decisive campaigns and battles of World War II have been dissected and subjected to the clear vision of hindsight. That hindsight became even sharper in 1974 with the British revelation of the *Ultra* secret.[2] Today, the critical decisions of another generation have been transformed into moves across the hexagonal spaces of the gaming board. Decisions that set thousands of men and machines into motion have been quantified and computerized. The fear, the elation, the mud, the flak, the hours spent peering into the terrible night, the sorrow, have now been transmuted into the bloodless roll of the war gamer's dice. Those dice roll through the clear summer skies of 1940 as the Royal Air Force and the Luftwaffe once again duel over Kent. They are scorched by the burning sands of North Africa as Rommel's Afrika Korps pushes the oft-defeated British toward a spot on the map named El Alamein. And they are caressed by the late afternoon wind off Saipan as Admiral Mitscher's carriers turn to launch against the fleeing Japanese fleet. Fascinated, perhaps, by the immensity of it all, the long-ago days of World War II continue to have a hold on modern imaginations and interests.

Almost unnoticed in the dramatic sweep of global war, a classic sea battle of maneuver, accurate gunnery, courage, and luck was fought in the damp, cold reaches of the North Pacific. It was a battle of which few people, other than naval officers and history buffs, have heard. It took place in a theatre of war of which most people have never heard. The sea battle fought off the Russian-owned Komandorski Islands on 26 March 1943 was a unique event in the forty-four month struggle between the Imperial Japanese Navy and the United States Navy. Neither airpower nor submarines played a part. It was fought entirely by daylight, making it the kind of traditional gunfire duel for which all the naval captains of the time were trained. When it was over, almost four hours after it began, an American force had escaped destruction at the hands of a Japanese force nearly twice its size. Incredibly, the Americans gave as good as they got. When the balance sheets were totted up, it was clear that the Americans had accomplished what they set out to do and the Japanese had not.

Like the theatre of war in which it occurred, the battle was of no consequence to the eventual outcome of the war. At best, it was a minor tactical victory for the United States Navy. It added luster to the career of some American naval officers and ended the career of a Japanese admiral. It eventually meant a difference of life or death to some infantrymen, Japanese and American alike. Even though it did not figure too importantly in the grand scale of World War II, for nearly four hours it was of the utmost importance to several thousand Japanese and American sailors. This is the story of that nearly forgotten fight.

CHAPTER 1

The Scene Is Set:
June 1942–March 1943

The Aleutian Islands are a chain lying roughly between 51° and 55° North Latitude and extending about 1,200 miles westward from the tip of the Alaskan Peninsula. Their northern position puts them on the shortest route between the United States and Japan. They are washed on their southern beaches by the North Pacific and on their northern shores by the Bering Sea. The islands are of volcanic origin, very mountainous, rather barren, and sparsely inhabited. From west to east, the principal islands are Attu, Kiska, Amchitka, Adak, and Unalaska. Because the warm Japanese Current meets cold Arctic air in the Aleutians, the islands are almost perpetually enshrouded in fog. They are also subject to an incredibly capricious, typhoon-like wind known as the williwaw.

The hazards to mariner and airmen alike are bad, even in an age of inertial guidance systems and other sophisticated aids to navigation. In 1942, the hazards were even worse. Charts were found to be inaccurate, and the airplanes of the day usually had to fly through, rather than over, the weather.

Given the state of the art in 1942 technology, the Aleutians seem an unlikely place to deliberately mount a military campaign. However, strategists with a global gaze rarely take notice of nature's constraints. In World War II, the lure of empire drove nations to fight in the trackless wastes of North Africa as well as in the fog and cold of the Aleutians. In both Japan and the United States, there were men who saw the bleak Aleutians as a potential path of invasion. Partly because of such views, Japan's effort to control the Pacific basin brought war to the Aleutians in June 1942.

The story has often been covered in detail, so this narrative will dwell only in a passing way on the course of events leading up to the Japanese attack on these islands. Briefly stated, the Japanese went to the Aleutians for three reasons: 1) The islands were seen as a possible route by which the Americans could attack the Home Islands. The practical difficulties of campaigning in the Aleutians made this the least valid reason of the three. 2) After the Doolittle raid of April 1942, the Japanese decided to establish a north-south patrol line that was to have Kiska as its northern anchor. This was probably the most militarily sound reason for going north. 3) Operations in the Aleutians were supposed to draw major American units away from the so-called decisive battle at Midway. Whatever merit this reason might have had was totally undermined by the successes of American cryptanalysts. As is well known, the United States Navy didn't take the proffered Aleutian bait and scored a decisive victory at Midway. After Midway, the least important reason for a Japanese outpost in the Aleutians suddenly seemed to be the most important. What began as a failed adjunct to a more important campaign assumed a momentum of its own.

If the Aleutian campaign is measured against the sweep of the German conquest of Europe or the American thrust across the Central Pacific, it is small change indeed. Strategic realities cannot conceal the fact that the war in that remote corner of the world drew many times more men and resources than necessity merited. In 1939, there were only two companies of United States Army infantry in the whole Alaskan area. By the summer of 1942, the total number of servicemen in the area was in the thousands and still climbing. Beginning in June 1942, and for the next thirty-eight months, Japanese and American servicemen fought one another, the weather, and intense boredom. Planners and logistics experts on both sides of the Pacific must have inwardly groaned in dismay as scant resources were shuttled off to the snowy environs of Attu and Adak.

In the end, the weight of the American effort proved too much for the Japanese. In May 1943, United States forces successfully invaded and captured Japanese-held Attu. Three months later, in August 1943, American and Canadian forces splashed ashore on Kiska only to find the enemy mysteriously gone. The fact that the Japanese no longer stood on American soil did not signal an end to the war in the north. From their Aleutian bases, American warships and bombers roamed farther westward to engage in pinprick raids on enemy bases in the Kurile Islands. The roar of the guns was finally stilled in August 1945. Like so many other arenas in which men had fought to the death, the Aleutians were quickly abandoned to the caprice of the fog and the williwaw. It had been a sideshow campaign that saw only three significant events in thirty-eight months of warfare. One was the fight for Attu, another was the adroitly managed evacuation of Kiska, and the last a unique sea battle. The land battle for Attu and the evacuation of Kiska are beyond the scope of this narrative. Before the story of the sea battle can be told, the reader is asked to return to the summer of 1942.

For the Japanese, the campaign began very nearly as scheduled. The planned air raids on the only American base of any consequence, Dutch Harbor, Unalaska Island, were carried out with only small loss to the Japanese. American resistance to the air raids was hampered by weather and uncertain leadership. The overall commander of American forces

7

in the Aleutian area was an admiral with the not-too-distinguished nickname of "Fuzzy." He chose to ignore the specific warning of Japanese intentions he received from Pearl Harbor and positioned his major naval units so far away from Dutch Harbor that they were out of the fight. Despite scant intelligence about the enemy's whereabouts, Army and Navy airmen strove courageously to strike the Japanese task force. No hits were scored, and several American planes were shot down or vanished forever into the leaden skies. On June 7, the enemy wrested the islands of Attu and Kiska from their "garrisons" of Aleuts, missionaries, and American naval weathermen. A Japanese landing was suspected when reports ceased coming in from the Kiska weather station. Confirmation of the Japanese presence was provided by the crew of a patrolling PBY.

Popular wisdom of the day held that Alaska was next on the Japanese timetable of invasion. Postwar investigation showed such fears to be false, but in the summer of 1942 they were real fears to many Americans. Myriad problems of distance, supply, and demands of other fighting fronts notwithstanding, American efforts were immediately dedicated to driving the invaders out. Bases closer to the enemy were established, first on Adak and later on Amchitka. From airbases on these islands, the Japanese were attacked at every opportunity. Army, Navy, and Canadian airmen pushed the technology of the day to the limits in an effort to keep a constant rain of bombs falling on the Japanese. They often succeeded, but often they did not. More than a few fliers took off into sunlit skies only to find their bases shrouded in impenetrable fog on their return. The airmen did manage to sink several enemy oilers, supply ships, and even a destroyer.

Not to be outdone, the surface navy tried its hand at bombarding the enemy in July and August. Fog thwarted the July effort, and the shoot in August provided indifferent results. Somewhat more productive were the submariners who chipped in by sinking a couple of merchantmen and two destroyers. The fights were not all one-sided, of course. Submarine USS *Grunion* was mined and lost with all hands while off Kiska. By using seaplanes, the Japanese managed to stage sporadic air raids on American bases. Adverse sea conditions cost them more aircraft than did American countermeasures. An RO-boat managed to torpedo the seaplane tender USS *Casco*, but was destroyed the next day. The bulk of the Japanese effort was concentrated on reinforcing and supplying their garrisons. In this endeavor, they were moderately successful. They were able to effect several sizeable movements of men between, and to, the islands by using warships as high-speed transports. Because the Japanese effort was perforce of smaller scale, the Americans suffered fewer losses to enemy action. The sputtering war of skirmish dragged on for six months, from June through December 1942. Neither side hurt the other too much, and no decisive clash of arms seemed to be in the offing. The new year brought with it a change of command on the American side and with it, a new, more decisive turn to the war.

As if war on the edge of the Arctic Circle didn't provide problems enough, the Americans spent the summer and fall of 1942 embroiled in a top-level command dispute. As previously noted, all arms in the Aleutian area were in the charge of a Navy man. Because of personality clashes with his subordinate commanders, friction soon developed. After several disputes over the location and establishment of new bases—disputes that had to be mediated from Washington—the man was relieved. Rear Admiral Thomas C. Kinkaid, a combat veteran well respected by his peers, took command in the Aleutians in January 1943. With him he brought Rear Admiral Charles H. McMorris to serve as task group commander of forces afloat. Admiral Kinkaid also brought with him a brief to begin planning a counterinvasion of Kiska. Before the plans could take real shape, a meeting half the world away scuttled the proposed attack. At the Casablanca Conference, America's British allies found such a diversion of effort unacceptable. The Kiska operation was therefore temporarily shelved as a sop to Allied harmony. Admiral Kinkaid was directed to continue planning and to concentrate his efforts on throttling the Japanese supply line. As with any island garrison, the enemy soldiers and marines on Attu and Kiska were dependent upon war materiel from home. Supplies for the Japanese defenders were shipped from the islands of Paramushiro and Shimushu, 650 miles to the west of Attu. It was a fragile link, and both sides recognized the fact.

In an effort to shatter the link, air attacks on the Japanese were stepped up. United States naval forces began to aggressively patrol astride the shipping lanes between Paramushiro and Attu. Amchitka Island, almost literally in the lap of the Kiska garrison, was occupied early in January. The increased level of American activity meant only one thing to the Japanese: an effort to oust the Aleutian garrisons was going to be mounted. Imperial Headquarters was moved to issue a directive that ordered the Aleutians held at all costs. The Army was directed to complete airfields on both Attu and Kiska no later than the end of March. It was an order that could not be carried out. Even after six months' occupation, the Japanese had been unable to construct the airfields upon which any reasonable hope of holding the islands depended.

In mid-February 1943, the dimly perceived threat of the future became reality to the Japanese. Admiral McMorris's task group conducted a bombardment of Attu on 18 February. When the shoot was finished, the light cruiser *Richmond*, heavy cruiser *Indianapolis*, and their escorting destroyers headed west in the hope of intercepting any incoming mechantmen. McMorris split his force into two groups, and as luck would have it, the *Indianapolis* did intercept a small merchantman inbound for Attu. The Arctic moon cast a cold, impassive light as the *Akagane Maru* was battered into junk and sent to a frigid grave. No survivors lived to tell the tale, but another Japanese ship was just over the horizon and heard the heavy booming of the guns. The ominous word that American warships were patrolling west of Attu soon reached Japanese headquarters. Even though another transport evaded the American patrol line and successfully unloaded at Kiska, further attempts were deemed too risky. The commander of Japan's Fifth Fleet, Vice Admiral Boshiro Hosogaya, decreed an end to surface transport. The man responsible for maintaining the Aleutian garrisons ordered that henceforth all supplies would be delivered by submarines.

The decision was quickly appealed by the Japanese Army, whose men formed the bulk of both garrisons. The arguments presented by the Army must have been persuasive, for Admiral Hosogaya agreed upon another try with surface ships. This time, though, there was a difference in the way the attempt was to be carried out. Instead of a single transport with little or no escort, a convoy was formed and provided with a heavy screen of warships. Operation A-GO was put into motion on 3 March, when the merchantmen and covering force put to sea, bound for Attu. The convoy made its run undetected and arrived in Holtz Bay, Attu, on 9 March. The cargo of food, ammo, and construction materiel was discharged, and all ships returned safely to Paramushiro.

Despite the success of Operation A-GO, the reality of the situation was plainly evident to the Japanese commanders. If they were to maintain their hold on Attu and Kiska, supplies had to be provided on a regular basis. Especially critical was the need for heavy construction equipment. Equally obvious was the fact that the success of one convoy was no guarantee that subsequent operations would also be successful. Admiral Hosogaya appears to have been a careful, cautious man. There is no way of knowing whether he would have tried to run another convoy to Attu as soon as he did. Cautious or not, his hand was soon forced. Within a few days of the A-GO convoy's return to base, a submarine brought an Army officer from Attu with an urgent request for another supply run. Food, and especially antiaircraft ammunition, were in short supply.

Perhaps his initial success emboldened the Japanese ad-

Vice Admiral Boshiro Hosogaya.   U.S. Navy

miral, for Hosogaya quickly issued the necessary orders. All warships available to him were again ordered to make ready for sea. Hosogaya knew his Fifth Fleet outnumbered American naval forces in the area. If the convoy was intercepted, an unexpectedly heavy covering force would be in a good position to destroy an American task group. The inevitable delay while the Americans replaced their losses would give the Army engineers on Attu and Kiska a respite in which to complete the vital airfields. Unknown to the Japanese admiral, the orders he issued in mid-March 1943 were about to precipitate a sea battle unique to the history of World War II.

World War II brought revolutionary technological, tactical, and strategic changes to warfare at sea. The most powerful blend of technology went to sea in the form of the modern aircraft carrier. The successful marriage of ship and airplane caused all tactical doctrines to be rewritten. It allowed strategic naval might to be projected far beyond the horizons of traditional Navy men. Dramatic as these changes proved to be, prior to the war they were ideas held only by a minority of naval officers. When the United States Navy went to war in 1941, its tactical doctrines, strategic theories, and technology were preponderantly rooted in tradition. Naval historian Samuel Eliot Morison has summed up the prewar Navy's idea of the future:

> Many senior officers of the navy envisaged the battles of the next war as long-range gunfire duels between battle lines, as at Jutland, an action so intensively studied at the Naval War College in Newport that one witty officer called Jutland "a major defeat of the United States Navy."[3]

During the 1920s and 1930s, the U.S. Navy had gained considerable experience in operating aircraft carriers. In November 1940, carrier aircraft of the British Royal Navy attacked the Italian battle fleet in the harbor at Taranto. It was a graphic demonstration of the striking power of the aircraft carrier. Nonetheless, most American admirals of 1941 still saw the epitome of naval power as a line of stately battleships pouring fire and destruction on the enemy. That traditional vision was destroyed forever on a bright Hawaiian morning in December 1941. The Imperial Japanese Navy sent its First Air Fleet ranging across the Pacific to destroy the American battle fleet as it lay at anchor. Three days later, Japanese land-based bombers sent the British battleship HMS *Prince of Wales* and the battlecruiser HMS *Repulse* to the bottom off Malaya.

THE SCENE IS SET

The final argument of the traditionalists, that no battleship able to defend itself by maneuver had ever been sunk by aircraft, went down with the British ships. The carriers under Admiral Chuichi Nagumo thereafter roamed at will across the Pacific and Indian oceans, forever consigning the traditional theories of naval power to the history books. They also consigned to the refuse heap the attitude held by most Western naval officers that the Japanese were a technically inept, imitative nation incapable of successfully fighting the U.S. Navy or the Royal Navy. These were lessons painfully and expensively learned.

The losses to the battle fleet effectively thrust the American carriers into the front rank. A meager fleet of carriers and cruisers was tasked with stemming the Japanese tide and preventing America's total defeat in the Pacific. Sorting out which tactics worked and which did not as they went, the carrier force launched Doolittle's bombers against Tokyo, checked the enemy advance in the Coral Sea, and tore the heart from the Japanese carrier force at Midway. This learning period was also not without cost. One by one, the six carriers initially available to the Pacific Fleet were whittled away through loss or damage. At one point, only a single American carrier was operational. So desperate was the situation that a carrier was temporarily borrowed from the Royal Navy. Fortunately, it was only a temporary expedient. Help *was* on the way.

By March 1943, an unprecedented frenzy of naval construction was under way in American shipyards. Scores of carriers were planned or on the building ways. Battleships, cruisers, destroyers, oilers, tenders, and landing craft were pouring from American shipyards. Thousands of young men were in the training programs destined to launch them from the decks of the carriers then building. By war's end, the United States Navy would have better than a hundred aircraft carriers of all classes. Pearl Harbor would be avenged many times over. All the expensively learned lessons of the early days were put to good use. Twenty-seven battleships were still in commission at war's end, but they no longer carried the banner for the fleet. Their job had become one of riding shotgun on the fast carriers or serving as bombardment ships with the amphibious forces.

It is in this context of change that the Battle of the Komandorski Islands must be viewed. Even though the speeds and ranges at which it was fought were representative of twentieth century technology, the style hearkened back to the earliest gun battles between ships. There was no carrier to be screened and protected from swarms of torpedo and dive bombers. The enemy was not a green blob on a radar screen or a dimly perceived shape looming out of the night. Instead, he was on the horizon, in plain sight, with his guns flashing. The familiar litany of *Fire, Splash, Spot*, taught in all the gunnery schools the world over, was the chant to which all movement was choreographed. It was no Jutland or Tsushima, but the officers of both sides were prepared by tradition and training to fight the battle. In his retelling of the Battle of Surigao Strait, where battleships fought battleships for the last time, Samuel Eliot Morison suggests that the ghosts of several famous admirals of antiquity may have been wistful onlookers. If that be so, it is likely that they also showed up to watch the Komandorski battle. It was one that they would surely understand.

THE JAPANESE—18–26 MARCH 1943

Admiral Hosogaya's response to the 18 March request by the Army for a supply run to Attu soon took shape. He had available two fast transports, the *Asaka Maru* and the *Sakito Maru*, and one slower ship, the *Sanko Maru*. Requisitions were issued, and soon the required supplies were being stowed in the holds of the transports. Since she had a speed of only 10 knots, Army-chartered *Sanko Maru* was ordered to sail ahead of the other two transports. This small merchantman sailed from the naval base at Kataoka, on the southwest coast of Shimushu, on 22 March. She was laden to her marks with

15

food, ammo, and building materiel. The destroyer *Usugumo* was rather grandly designated 2nd Escort Force and sent with her. These two ships were directed to proceed to a rendezvous area approximately 60 miles due south of the Russian-owned Komandorski Islands. The other transports and the main escort force would meet them there on the morning of 25 March. The location of the rendezvous area was chosen by Admiral Hosogaya because experience showed it to be beyond the normal radius of American PBYs flying from Adak.

A second group, designated D Convoy, and comprising the light cruiser *Abukuma*, the destroyers *Ikazuchi* and *Inazuma*, and the other two transports, left Kataoka on 23 March. Because the *Asaka Maru* had been impressed into the Imperial Navy and outfitted as an auxiliary cruiser, she was used mainly as a personnel transport. On this trip, the Attu garrison commander was among the 550 Army men on board. The other transport in D Convoy, the *Sakito Maru*, was deeply laden with several antiaircraft guns, food, ammo, and lumber. There had recently been an epidemic of typhoid fever aboard, so she carried no troops. The convoy commander was Rear Admiral Tomoichi Mori, who had his flag in the *Abukuma*. The convoy group was followed to sea later in the day when the heavy cruiser *Nachi* let go her last line and led the heavy cruiser *Maya*, the light cruiser *Tama*, and the destroyers *Wakaba* and *Hatsushimo* out to meet the swell of the deep Pacific.

Japanese Forces Involved in the Convoy to Attu 23 March
1943

Fifth Fleet (Northern Force): Vice Admiral Hosogaya
    Heavy cruisers: *Nachi* (F), *Maya* (CruDiv 1)
    Light cruiser: *Tama*
    Destroyers: *Wakaba, Hatsushimo* (DesDiv 21)
D Convoy: Rear Admiral Tomoichi Mori (ComDesRon 1)
    Light cruiser: *Abukuma* (F)
    Destroyers: *Ikazuchi, Inazuma* (DesDiv 6)
    Transports: *Asaka Maru, Sakito Maru*

Admiral Hosogaya's flagship, the heavy cruiser *Nachi*.   U.S. Navy

THE SCENE IS SET

2nd Escort Force
  Destroyer: *Usugumo*
  Transport: *Sanko Maru*

The eight fast, well-armed warships under Admiral Hosogaya's flag constituted a powerful fighting force. All were materially equal, if not superior, to comparable ships in the American Navy. All had served in the vast initial rush of conquest. Both of the heavy cruisers and all the destroyers had participated in the invasion of the Dutch East Indies. The *Nachi*, *Ikazuchi*, and *Inazuma* fought in the Battle of the Java Sea. In the closing stages of that chaotic battle, the *Nachi*'s gunfire contributed to the sinking of HMS *Exeter*, the British heavy cruiser made famous by the Battle of the River Plate. The *Abukuma* participated in the invasions of Kavieng and Rabaul and went with Admiral Nagumo's carriers on the raid into the Indian Ocean. All eight participated in the Aleutian operations of June 1942. With the exception of the *Maya*, *Ikazuchi*, and *Inazuma*, all remained in northern waters in the months thereafter. After a short stay in Japan, the *Maya* and the two destroyers were dispatched to the South Pacific as the fleet responded to the American landing on Guadalcanal. Like so many other ships that were thrown into the Guadalcanal crucible, both the *Maya* and *Ikazuchi* were scorched by war's fiery blast. The destroyer was first hit by artillery fire from Tulagi Island and then badly damaged on the night of 12–13 November 1942 during the naval battle of Guadalcanal. The next day, a shot-down American bomber crashed into the *Maya*. Both ships were soon on their way to Japan, accompanied by the *Inazuma*, which was squadron mate to the *Ikazuchi*. After completion of repairs, all three were once again assigned to Hosogayas's Fifth Fleet. American cryptanalysts had become fairly adept at keeping track of Japanese naval movements by this time, but they completely missed the *Maya*'s move to Fifth Fleet. Her presence in the North Pacific would soon prove to be an unexpected and unpleasant surprise to some American sailors.[4]

18

Like all the heavy cruisers built for the Imperial Navy, both the *Nachi* and *Maya* were formidable products of the naval architect's art. They were well armored, rated at 34 knots, heavily armed with a main battery of ten 8-inch guns, and each mounted sixteen torpedo tubes. They were among the first heavy cruisers built; the *Nachi* entered service in 1929 and the *Maya* in 1932. Both had been modernized before the war. The light cruisers *Abukuma* and *Tama* were relatively elderly ships, both having entered service in the early 1920s. The destroyers with Hosogaya were all modern ships completed in the 1930s. All of the Japanese ships were liberally armed with torpedoes, a weapon used with devastating effectiveness by the Imperial Navy.[5] Unlike their American adversaries, none of the Japanese ships were equipped with radar.

Ships do not sail or fight themselves, of course. In their men, the ships of Fifth Fleet were well served. The officers and sailors of the Imperial Navy were second to none in discipline and fighting spirit. Fitness, simplicity, martial ardor, and a uniquely Japanese willingness to die in battle were the hallmarks of the Imperial Navy. Where other prewar navies engaged in artificial, set-piece drills, the Japanese practiced under the most arduous, war-like conditions possible. So severe was this prewar training that historian Arthur Marder reports at least one Japanese officer voiced the opinion that actual combat was easier.[6] By 26 March 1943, Japan had been at war with the United States for sixteen months. The first harbingers of defeat had been experienced at Midway and Guadalcanal. Nonetheless, the Imperial Navy was uncowed. The Fifth Fleet was a well-equipped, experienced force tempered by war. In all respects, it was a formidable enemy.

A falling barometer gave warning, leaving no one surprised to see a bad storm making up on the morning of 24 March. Soon the high wind and towering seas forced all three groups to reduce speed. As a weather-punished, gloomy dawn broke on the morning of the 25th, the bridge watch on the ships in D Convoy were just able to make out the snow-topped mass of Bering Island, the largest of the Komandorskis. The convoy then turned south and met Admiral Hosogaya's covering force at the rendezvous area around 1600. As the two groups converged, a signal light flashed through the gloom as the flagship ordered the force into column. Pagoda-masted *Nachi* took the van, followed by the *Maya*, *Tama*, *Wakaba*, *Hatsushimo*, *Abukuma*, *Ikazuchi*, *Asaka Maru*, and *Sakito Maru*, with *Inazuma* bringing up the rear. Fifth Fleet and D Convoy now formed a column some two miles long. The methodical sweep of the lookouts quickly established that the *Sanko Maru* and *Usugumo* had not yet made the rendezvous. Admiral Hosogaya rightly assumed that they had been delayed by the adverse weather and changed the rendezvous time to 0600, 26 March. A message to that effect was sent out to the missing ships.

The night of 25–26 March was one of waiting as the ten Japanese ships steamed back and forth along a sixty-mile-long, north-south line fixed through the tip of Bering Island. The storm that had disrupted Hosogaya's plan abated through the night, but 0600 came and went without any sign of the *Sanko Maru* or the *Usugumo*. Around 0730 on the morning of the 26th, a column turn was signaled from the *Nachi*'s bridge. The Japanese ships, which were on the southern end of their waiting line, one by one began to put their helms over and once again plod back toward the north. Sunrise was not expected for nearly another hour, although the long predawn twilight provided just enough light to see. As the *Asaka Maru*'s helmsman steadied her up on the new course, the constant sweep of the starboard lookout's binoculars suddenly stopped as they touched the southern horizon. Pencil-like in its slenderness, a mast was just discernible at the line where sky met water.

When the lookout's report rang out, a feeling of relief went over the cold bridge watch standers. With the *Sanko Maru* and the *Usugumo* at last joining up, the convoy could finally stop the tiresome plodding back and forth and get on with the dash to Attu. Relief was short-lived. Watching eyes began to widen as one mast, then another, and another, began to march over the horizon. There were far too many to be the missing Japanese ships. It took but another minute to recognize them for what they were—American warships! The brisk clatter of signal light shutters was soon heard as an urgent warning signal was flashed to the *Abukuma*. For a flagship, the performance of the *Abukuma*'s signal and bridge watch was not too satisfactory. They not only took fifteen minutes to acknowledge the *Asaka Maru*'s signal, but also reported to the *Nachi* that the missing Japanese ships were in sight. The *Inazuma* performed better, accurately reporting that enemy warships were in sight.

The masts were also sighted by one of Admiral Hosogaya's staff officers, Commander Kintaro Miura. Like the others, his first impression was that the approaching ships were the Japanese stragglers. He reported his sighting to the admiral and raised his binoculars to continue studying the distant vessels. When the fighting top of a light cruiser began to show, it was obvious that a rendezvous of a different sort had taken place. The insistent clamor of the general alarm began to sound through the Japanese ships. It called men from hammocks, from the head, from warm galleys. Its urgent message was quickly made known—Yankees in sight!

By flag hoist and signal light, orders flowed from the *Nachi*'s bridge in rapid-fire sequence. The two marus and the destroyers *Ikazuchi* and *Inazuma* were directed to clear off to the northwest. Admiral Mori's flagship, along with the other two destroyers, was ordered to form on the *Nachi*. Speed was increased and the fleet ordered into a sweeping turn to the southwest. Admiral Hosogaya's intention was to get the Fifth Fleet between the Americans and their airbases on Adak and Amchitka. If the American task force could be forced to the west, it might be possible to destroy them before land-based bombers could interfere. As the coming day lighted the sky, the American ships were counted and accurately identified. One *Omaha*-class light cruiser, one *Pensacola*-class heavy cruiser, and first five, but later four, destroyers were counted. Hoso-

21

gaya's insistence on making use of all the warships available to him seemed about to pay off. The heavy units of Fifth Fleet outnumbered the Americans two to one.

As his cruisers bore down on the Americans, Admiral Hosogaya ordered the *Ikazuchi* and the *Inazuma* to leave the transports and join the main body. He also ordered his flagship to get her spotting planes airborne. The two transports, meanwhile, steamed to the northwest until the Komandorskis came into sight. There they came upon the *Usugumo* steaming full tilt toward the action. Although the Japanese destroyer captain was following the universal military dictum of heading toward the sound of the guns, his admiral ordered the destroyer to remain with the *Sanko Maru*. All four of these ships were eventually ordered to return to Kataoka.

THE AMERICANS—14–26 MARCH

In mid-March, Admiral Kinkaid ordered Rear Admiral McMorris to patrol the western approaches to Attu. Kinkaid had been advised by Naval Intelligence that the Japanese were going to run a convoy into Attu. He was also motivated by the knowledge that his 3 March suggestion to substitute an assault on Attu for the one on Kiska had been approved. The land forces and shipping available on the west coast of the United States were just sufficient to carry out the smaller assault envisioned. Since it promised to be an operation that would be carried out on a shoestring, any possible reduction in the odds facing the American landing force was welcome. Stopping the reinforcement of the Attu garrison was one obvious way to lower the odds.

Even though his task group was incomplete, Admiral McMorris decided to tune up the ships available with a battle practice. Breaking his flag in the *Richmond*, he left Dutch Harbor on 14 March. The *Richmond* was accompanied by the destroyers *Bailey*, *Coghlan*, and *Bancroft*. Under McMorris's watchful eye, all four ships spent the day and night exercising at various gunnery and torpedo drills. Charles McMorris was

USS *Richmond*, November 1942.   National Archives

known as a hard taskmaster, so it is no surprise to read in his report that he thought the exercise was unsatisfactory. Regardless, operational demands remained in effect. All four ships returned to Dutch Harbor on the morning of the 15th. After refueling, the *Richmond* followed the *Bailey* and the *Coghlan* back to sea, bound for Adak. McMorris's small force was designated Task Group 16.6.

On 16 March, the *Richmond* and her consorts slipped into Kuluk Bay, Adak, to top off with fuel. Her Deck Log shows that 1,300 barrels of oil were needed to send the *Richmond* on her way. By 1908, the task group was under way again, headed for its patrol area. McMorris wrote in his Action Report that his February experience led him to decide on a patrol to the northwest of Attu and as far west as 168°-00′E. In fact, it was intelligence information that ultimately dictated the patrol area. The three American ships were southwest of Kiska by midday on Sunday, the 21st. At 1240, the general alarm sent the men to their battle stations. A few minutes later, a *Jake* scout plane came into view. The Japanese shadower ventured close enough for the *Richmond* to fling forty rounds of 3-inch antiaircraft fire at it, but the only effect was to exercise the gun crews. The plane did retire to a more discreet range, but by 1327, had closed enough for the *Bailey* to try her hand at shooting it down. The snooper again escaped unscathed. Japanese records state that American naval forces were known to be operating around Attu, so it is almost certain that Admiral Hosogaya was informed of this sighting. A welcome addition was made to the meager strength of Task Group 16.6 on the morning of 22 March. In the vicinity of 50° − 59′N, 173° − 16′E, an area due south of Attu, the heavy cruiser *Salt Lake City* and the destroyers *Dale* and *Monaghan* joined up.

Task Group 16.6 as of 1200 22 March 1943

CTG 16.6: Rear Admiral Charles H. McMorris, USN

    Heavy cruiser: *Salt Lake City* (CA 25) Captain Bertram J. Rodgers, USN

24

Light cruiser: *Richmond* (CL 9) Captain Theodore Waldschmidt, USN
ComDesRon 14: Captain Ralph Riggs, USN
   Destroyers: *Bailey* (DD 492) Lieutenant Commander John
            Atkeson, USN
            Coghlan (DD 606) Commander Benjamin
            Tompkins, USN
            Dale (DD 353) Commander Anthony Ror-
            schach, USN
            Monaghan (DD 354) Lieutenant Com-
            mander Peter Horn, USN
   The *Salt Lake City* had departed Pearl Harbor on 11 March,
rendezvoused with the destroyers on the morning of the 17th,
and entered Dutch Harbor that same afternoon. Upon her
arrival, she immediately went alongside the oiler *Guadalupe* to
refuel. Lieutenant George O'Connell, the assistant gunnery
officer, describes what happened after the *Salt Lake City*'s arrival:

> Suddenly, we became aware that our arrival was a festive oc-
> casion. We were deluged with swarms of visitors, both official
> and unofficial—officers and enlisted, line and staff, Sea Bees,
> Coast Guard and Army. The official visitors were somber,
> impersonal, quietly efficient. They delivered briefings, plans,
> instructions, documents, and charts. The unofficial visitors were
> gregarious, curious, and excited. The atmosphere seemed charged
> with excitement and high expectation. Everyone seemed to
> expect something was about to happen and *Salt Lake City* was
> going to cause it to happen.[7]

One section at a time, for only four hours apiece, the *Salt Lake
City*'s sailors were granted liberty. The contrast between the
tropical lushness of Pearl Harbor and bleak Dutch Harbor was
profound. Lieutenant O'Connell again:

> We found the station to be muddy with wet slush, but the
> mountain slopes surrounding the station were covered with
> clean . . . snow. The station resembled a frontier village with
> one-story wooden buildings and three-story wooden barracks.

USS *Salt Lake City*, taken at Dutch Harbor, 29 March 1943. Courtesy Ben Johnston

Sea Bees and elaborate heavy construction equipment was everywhere. SOC aircraft flew overhead pulling target sleeves for antiaircraft training. The "Longest Bar in the World" was found at the Officer's Club. An elaborate Navy Exchange was opened . . . as was the "Waterfront Saloon." A land-office business was going on everywhere.[8]

For those without the time or the inclination to go ashore, a memorandum to all hands offered a $5.00 prize to the man catching the biggest fish. The night before the ship was scheduled to leave Dutch Harbor, a few of her officers got up a poker game at the Officer's Club. Lieutenant Commander Windsor Gale, the first lieutenant, won one pot with a hand of aces and eights. As he raked in the chips, he made the traditional remark about it being "a dead man's hand." No one laughed. A week later it proved to be a prophetic remark.[9]

These temporary idylls were left behind on the afternoon of the 19th, when the ship left Dutch Harbor. She was again accompanied by the *Dale* and the *Monaghan*. Following in McMorris's wake, they stopped at Adak just long enough to refuel and again headed west. Despite roughening seas, the *Salt Lake City* and her escorts made the rendezvous as scheduled. The advent of newer, more capable ships was making this pioneer cruiser into something of a technical antique, but McMorris was no doubt glad to have the long reach of her ten 8-inch guns in his task group.

One of the so-called treaty cruisers, the *Salt Lake City* slid down the ways of the New York Shipbuilding Company on 23 January 1929. Numerically the second ship of a two-ship class of heavy cruisers, she was the first launched. Initially armed with ten 8-inch guns, four 5-inch guns, six 21-inch torpedo tubes, manned by some 560 officers and men, she was considered a powerful unit. She was gleaming with the shine of newness and polished brightwork when she hosted President Hoover, the Secretary of the Navy, and the Chief of Naval Operations in May 1930. She continued to gleam, but the fame of being first passed, as bigger, better-protected

USS *Dale*, May 1944.   National Archives

classes of cruisers were commissioned into the Navy. She gained a reputation as a bad roller and a very wet ship. Because her builders had to work within a treaty-imposed limit of 10,000 tons, she was lightly constructed and by later standards, lightly armored. Somewhere along the line, Navy men began to refer to her as a "tinclad." The ship nevertheless established a reputation for excellence in all fields: the *Salt Lake City* was tops in engineering performance, scored the highest number of points ever scored by a cruiser in torpedo drills, had an outstanding aviation detachment, and excelled in fleet sports competition. A tradition of excellence and loyalty to the ship was established, which was impressed on every man who joined her crew. A spirit that no job was impossible, that all material deficiencies could be overcome, was fostered and nurtured through the decade of the thirties. It was with this spirit that she went to war.[10]

Thanks to Captain Ellis M. Zacharias, her skipper when war broke out, the *Salt Lake City*'s crew had already begun to make the important mental transition from peace to war. Zacharias was an intense, cerebral student of Japanese affairs. His interest in Japan and his involvement in the effort to crack Japanese military codes caused him to be one of the many men who believed war with Japan was imminent. His expectation of war therefore led him to begin preparing his crew months before the attack on Pearl Harbor. During the summer of 1941, the *Salt Lake City* escorted a Dutch merchantman loaded with crated fighter planes to Java. Zacharias was well aware of the tense political situation and evidently feared the possibility of Japanese interference. He issued orders that should any unidentified plane approach the ship, the antiaircraft battery officer on watch had permission to open fire on his own volition. It was a startling order to men grown used to the strictures of peacetime routine. From that point on, the *Salt Lake City* was essentially on a wartime footing. She was at sea when the blow fell on Pearl Harbor. One of her former officers

USS *Monaghan.* National Archives

USS *Bailey*, 12 December 1942.   National Archives

remembers experiencing a feeling of outrage, not so much with the Japanese, but with the ships caught so unprepared.

The losses to the battle fleet meant that the *Salt Lake City* and the other heavy cruisers had to shoulder the operational burdens that might otherwise have been carried by the battleships. As a consequence, the *Salt Lake City* was a busy ship throughout the first year of the war. She was off Wotje Island in the Marshalls chain in February 1942, where she fired what her historian feels were the first American shells to fall on Japanese-held territory. Later the same month, she bombarded the former American base on Wake Island. In April, she accompanied the carrier *Hornet* to Tokyo with the Doolittle raiders. Her lookouts were the first to sight the Japanese patrol boat that caused Doolittle and his men to be launched earlier than planned. In August, she was part of the task force off Guadalcanal as the United States Navy made the first of many amphibious assaults to come. In September, she was in the company of the carrier *Wasp* when that ship was torpedoed. Some of the *Wasp*'s survivors were transferred to the *Salt Lake City*'s deck by the rescuing destroyers. On the night of 11–12 October 1942, she fought in the savage, almost point-blank melee off Cape Esperance, Guadalcanal. When the light cruiser *Boise* unwisely turned on her searchlights, the Japanese obligingly began to shoot her to pieces. Captain Ernest G. Small, the *Salt Lake City*'s second wartime skipper, unselfishly interposed his ship between the enemy and the flaming *Boise*. Ten gun salvos flamed out from the *Salt Lake City* with well-drilled precision and accuracy. She slammed hits into the Japanese heavy cruiser *Furutaka* that ultimately proved fatal. The *Swayback Maru*, as the *Salt Lake City* came to be known, paid a price for her gallantry.[11] Three major hits and an ensuing fire necessitated a return to Pearl Harbor. Though the repair job was not originally supposed to take long, the ship was in yard hands from 1 November 1942 until 1 March 1943.

While in Pearl Harbor Navy Yard, the once clean ship became filthy as layer upon layer of peacetime paint and cork

USS *Coghlan*, June 1943.   National Archives

insulation were scraped and chipped from every bulkhead. The dirt had to be endured because combat experience showed the cork and layers of paint to be an extreme fire hazard. In addition to damage repairs, several official and unofficial alterations were made to the ship. Her internal communications were improved by the addition of sound-powered phones. These replaced the "unofficial" system her gunners had rigged as a backup to the unreliable dial-type phones originally fitted. A rudimentary Combat Information Center, an integral part of newer ships, was rigged in a corner of her charthouse. An "unofficial" stable element was added to her 5-inch battery fire-control system. New rangekeepers were installed in both main battery control stations. A visit to the Submarine Base by one of her officers provided four small, mechanical rangekeepers known as Baby Fords. These were installed in her 8-inch turrets. Her gunnery officer managed to have the yard install a backup to the compressed air system that cleaned the gun bores between rounds. A continual and potentially catastrophic problem of loss of rudder control caused the engineers to home-build a backup steering system that was powered by a "liberated" diesel engine.

These weren't the only alterations to the *Salt Lake City*. Even before war's outbreak, she had landed her torpedo tubes and added four more 5-inch guns. Unlike newer designs, her 5-inch guns were in open mounts, with no gun house to protect the crews from muzzle blast, spray, or flying shrapnel. Six quadruple 40-mm mounts and nineteen 20-mm guns were mounted on her decks and superstructure to counter the threat from the air. Her gun directors and masts also bore witness to a new branch of technology in the form of radar antennae mounted thereon. Like all American cruisers, she carried float-equipped scouting planes and two large catapults with which to launch them. A 1940 refit had improved crew accommodations by replacing hammocks with bunks, but a wartime crew of 1,250 officers and men meant that the ship was very crowded. Some men chose to escape the claustrophobic effect of the berthing spaces by bedding down in the same compartments where they worked. Others had no choice; photos of one space reveal a row of desks with a row of neatly triced bunks opposite. The continual addition of weight in equipment, guns, ammo, stores, and men had caused the top of her armor belt, once three feet above the waterline, to be awash. The added topweight made her somewhat tender in a roll and meant that in any kind of a seaway, her low-lying waist was perpetually awash. She was crowded, overweight, slower than in her youth, obsolescent, but still needed. Nothing could be done about her basic deficiencies, but the ship that left Pearl Harbor on 11 March 1943 was materially improved as a fighting unit.

There were many changes in personnel as well. Captain Small left the ship in January 1943. He was relieved by Captain Bertram J. Rodgers, a tall handsome officer who wore both submariner's dolphins and aviator's wings on his breast. Rodgers was a 1916 graduate of Annapolis who had command experience in both submarines and destroyers. He had also served in the airships *Los Angeles*, *Akron*, and *Macon*. He left the latter the day before she crashed. He went to *Salt Lake City* after a year's duty on the staff of Admiral Ernest J. King. Unlike the reserved Captains Small and Zacharias, he was a frequent visitor to the wardroom, a fact appreciated by his officers. He has been described by several of his former officers as a good golfer, a good poker player, and an admirable man. His outgoing personality, lack of guile, and obvious professional competence quickly gained him acceptance with his crew.[12]

Captain Rodgers had been preceded by a new executive officer, Commander Worthington S. Bitler, who went on board in November 1942. Worthy Bitler graduated from Annapolis in 1922. He was an avid fisherman and was known as a strict administrator. A hard worker, his cap set at a rakish tilt, he took his responsibilities in earnest. He openly admits that he was a hard-nosed, demanding officer, but he is also proud of

Captain Bertram Rodgers, CO of the *Salt Lake City*, 26 March 1943. Courtesy Worthy Bitler

the fact that he was always willing to give a man another chance. He preferred to settle disciplinary problems in such a way that no entry was required in a man's record. This is an assertion that is borne out by others who served under him. He was also a lifelong amateur artist who later designed a coat of arms for the *Salt Lake City*. He characteristically declined to take the credit for this, preferring to remain anonymous. Since he had transferred from the *Pensacola*, sister ship to the *Salt Lake City*, he had no trouble finding his way around.

Commander W. S. "Worthy" Bitler, Rodgers's
exec.   Courtesy Worthy Bitler

Thirty-eight years later, Rodgers would say that he ". . . was damn lucky to have Bitler."[13]

Also new to the *Salt Lake City* was Father Richard Hodge. The tall, red-haired Franciscan priest joined the Navy early in 1942 because, in his words, "It was the only fight going." Articulate and outspoken, he was almost literally dragooned into the ship's company by Captain Rodgers. Father Hodge was stationed in Pearl Harbor, awaiting assignment to a ship, when the *Salt Lake City* came in from Guadalcanal. His intro-

37

duction to Rodgers was roundabout but effective. While at Sunday Mass late in February 1943, Rodgers suddenly turned to the other *Salt Lake City* men with him and asked, "How about this guy for our chaplain?" A devout Catholic who attended Mass as often as he could, Rodgers was determined to have the priest on board his ship when she left Pearl Harbor. Since time was short, and to the astonishment of Father Hodge, a car called for him the next day and delivered him to the foot of the *Salt Lake City*'s gangplank. Within hours of a pleasant lunch with Rodgers, Father Hodge had orders to the ship. In less than a month, the priest was to make an impression on the crew that remains strong over forty years later.[14]

Other personnel changes were less salutary. The needs of a rapidly expanding Navy saw 50 percent of the *Salt Lake City*'s enlisted personnel transferred to new construction. In keeping with ship's policy, the men transferred were not the duds, as is often common practice in the service. It was ship's policy to reward good performance; the transferees were men who had performed well and who hadn't been home for some time. As attrition in the Fire Control Division approached 70 percent, George O'Connell felt compelled to approach the gun boss, Lieutenant Commander Jim Brewer, about the loss of so many experienced men. Brewer heard his assistant out and then reminded him of the old adage that nobody is irreplaceable. O'Connell was forced to retort, "Everybody all at once is irreplaceable!" His concern was understandable; no manager likes to see a winning team broken up. In this case, the difference between winning and losing the game could very well mean the difference between life or death. Brewer remembers that after this meeting, he brought the problem to the attention of Captain Rodgers and the transfers were thereafter halted.

In his account of the Komandorski battle, Samuel Eliot Morison attaches great significance to the high percentage of turnover in the *Salt Lake City*'s crew. On the surface, it would seem that the ship might be critically hampered in her fighting ability. It certainly was not a good situation, but for three reasons was not as bad as it seemed. To begin with, the crew had been largely unchanged during the first year of war. The men had cross-trained extensively within their departments. In the gunnery chain, for example, everyone from rangefinder operators to control personnel, from rammermen in the turrets to powdermen in the magazines, was capable of doing two or three jobs. The policy of extensive cross-training was followed throughout the ship. As men were transferred out, the next most experienced man was put into the vacated position. The critical positions in gunnery control, at the guns, and in the fire and engine rooms remained filled with men who had some experience at the job. The high caliber of the *Salt Lake City's* senior petty officers is exemplified by the way one of her turret officers describes his enlisted turret captain:

> Chief Turret Captain Virgil Brandon was the textbook example of a Chief Petty Officer and leader. Under him, the turret part of my division ran virtually in automatic control. His turret crew was the fastest and best in the ship, never missing a buzzer, and never giving me the slightest concern in battle or out.[15]

All evidence points to the fact that Chief Brandon's performance was the norm throughout the *Salt Lake City*. The confidence imparted to young, green sailors just out of boot camp by men like Chief Brandon was one of several steadying influences at work on the new men.

Another factor that ameliorated the effect of the many transfers was that the *Salt Lake City's* corps of experienced officers was left largely intact. Many had been on board since before the war. Their numbers included Naval Academy graduates, reservists, and men commissioned from the ranks. In addition to those men already mentioned, the ranks of experienced officers included Lieutenants J. F. B. Johnston, Bob Matusek, and Jerry Engle in the turrets. In the gunnery control chain were Lieutenants Lyle Ramsey, George Halvorsen, Chet Lee, Howard Grahn, Lieutenant (jg) Gerry Reeves, and Marine Major Bob Taplett. Jim Brewer later wrote of Lyle Ramsey: "He could solve the gunnery problems in his head as well as the director could. I always felt that he worked the thing as a toy merely to check on what he already knew to be the answer."[16] Damage control was well served by men like Lieutenant (jg) Bill Hosey and Ensign Jim Mew. The ship's chief engineer, Commander Ted Kobey, would soon find out how fortunate he was to have Ensign Vince Dahlen in charge of the after engine room. Like Jim Mew, Dahlen was a former warrant officer recently commissioned.

These men were seasoned officers, tested by a year of combat. They were serious about their business, had grown confident in their abilities, and were knit together by pride in their ship. They no longer made mistakes like the one at Wake Island when the ship was put onto a bombardment course that put the sun in the gunner's eyes. The adverse effects of all the transfers on combat savvy were therefore all but offset. All the critical positions in control, the turrets, and the engineering spaces were under the supervision of experienced, combat-wise officers and petty officers.

The last factor ameliorating the effect of the transfers was the strong tradition of excellence present among all the old hands. It was not something that could be taught from a training manual. Nevertheless, the constant expectation of high performance was a tangible presence in shipboard life. One of the most obvious goads to good performance among the gunners was the presence of a forty-seven-man Marine detachment among the ship's company. The Marines were under the command of Major Bob Taplett, and among their duties was the manning of two of the 5-inch guns and several of the 40-mm and 20-mm mounts. The rivalry between sailors and Marines is no secret. As Taplett points out, it was conspicuous in the *Salt Lake City*:

> The traditional rivalry . . . was manifest daily, especially in gunnery excellence. In the Fleet Gunnery Competition during

A group of the *Salt Lake City*'s officers at Mare Island Navy Yard, April 1943. *Front row, left to right:* LCDR Jim Brewer, the gun boss; Bitler; CAPT Rodgers; CDR Loftin, the medical officer; LCDR David D. Hawkins, the navigator; *back row, left to right:* LCDR Lindsey, 1st lieutenant; LT Pugsley, the communications officer; LT Lambert; LT Letterman, supply officer. Courtesy Worthy Bitler

summer and fall 1941, the two Marine 5-inch crews and I as Battery Officer outscored the . . . Navy 5-inch crews in local control firing excellence. . . . The Marines never let the sailors forget who was Number One at the Navy's own game. This rivalry continued when the Marines were assigned to the 40-mm and the 20-mm.

Taplett also remembers the loyalty his men felt toward the ship:

Once ashore, the sailors and Marines of the *Salt Lake City* always stood together as a shipboard unit when it involved the ship's reputation vis-a-vis another ship. The *Salt Lake City* had one of the best trained, integrated, and cohesive crews as compared to some of the other ship's crews observed in my experience.[17]

As the *Salt Lake City* prepared to leave Pearl Harbor in the waning days of February 1943, she was not as sharp a fighting unit as she had been the preceding November. Although not exactly a rookie either, her officers recognized the need to restore the fighting edge so much in evidence at Cape Esperance.

From 20 thru 24 February, the ship's company was fully occupied provisioning, loading the magazines, and refueling the ship. On 25 February, she put to sea and immediately began an arduous schedule of drill. Before Captain Rodgers's wish that the ship ". . . shoot, shoot, shoot . . . ," could be implemented, however, one serious problem had to be dealt with. A few of the *Salt Lake City*'s men maintain that the largely inexperienced work force at Pearl Harbor Navy Yard caused nearly as much damage as it fixed. Some of those complaints are borne out by what happened the first time the ship made ready to exercise the main battery. The director trained on the target sled, the turrets were cast loose and told to match pointers with the director. Gun boss Jim Brewer waited for the turrets to cease training and then stepped to the wind screen to make his customary check on whether the turrets bore as directed. To his complete surprise, all he saw was the backs of the turrets! Even though the main battery had been aligned prior to departure, last-minute work by the yard resulted in the director and turrets being switched together 180° out of synchronization.[18]

Capable hands soon put the problem right and many young men thereafter heard the thunder of heavy guns for the first time. Main, secondary, and automatic weapon batteries were put through their paces. They fired at target sleds, towed sleeves, and drone aircraft. An unsuccessful attempt was even made to down a drone aircraft by firing a predicted barrage with the main battery. The newly constituted CIC team worked hard at tracking and plotting multiple targets. Exercises were conducted with a submarine to familiarize new lookouts with the sight of a periscope coursing through the water.

The many drills and exercises caused more than a few defects in the work done by the Navy Yard to show up. After a week, the ship returned to Pearl Harbor. Captain Rodgers and his officers would have liked more time to train in the quiet of the Hawaiian operating area, but operational orders were in effect. On 11 March, the ship departed Pearl Harbor for the Aleutians. Although not ideal, the assignment to the Aleutians was known to be temporary and was considered an acceptable opportunity to drill the ship back into topnotch fighting shape. Nobody on board expected to be put to the test as soon as he was.

There were a good many similarities between the *Salt Lake City* and the *Richmond.* The light cruiser was built in Philadelphia, just across the Delaware River from where the *Salt Lake City* was built. She commissioned in 1923, supposedly to serve in the role of a fast scouting cruiser. Her slender, four-stacked silhouette resembled nothing so much as an oversized four-piper destroyer. By the time she went to war, she was totally obsolete. She carried a fairly large main battery of ten 6-inch guns, but had no stable element in the fire control system. She had no main battery plotting room, only a rude CIC, an inadequate secondary battery of 3-inch guns, and six torpedo tubes. Like the *Salt Lake City*, she carried catapult-launched spotting planes, and was newly burdened with radar and automatic antiaircraft guns. The effect on her men of her obvious obsoleteness was to foster a strong spirit of "make do." As an example, her first radar outfit was installed largely by her own men. They had to refer continually to the technical manuals provided by the manufacturer, but soon the radar was installed, tuned, and in operation. Also in common with the *Salt Lake City*, her men had endured the laborious job of stripping the ship of her layers of peacetime paint and inflammable cork insulation.[19]

Wartime additions of equipment and the increased need for watch standers doubled the size of her crew. There were some 800 men crammed into her slim hull, an influx that

43

drastically changed the old style of life. Electrician's Mate 1c George Ales, on board since 1937, tells of the change:

> When your mates returned from a night on the beach to discuss their adventures with you, they usually brought food along to help the conversation. After the influx of reservist and civilian type sailors, that sort of close bound [feeling] didn't exist any more. You kept your locker locked; no more coming off watch and opening your locker to find a note, "George, I borrowed your white hat . . . also I owe you a couple of bucks next payday."[20]

The *Richmond* served as flagship of the Pacific Submarine Force during the 1930s, a period that saw her acquire a reputation as a taut, spit-and-polish ship. War causes most spit and polish to quickly disappear, but the *Richmond* was still tautly run, a fact attested to by Coxswain Jim Turner:

> The Executive Officer was as strict an officer as I ever served under. He wrote a ship's company book of all the Do's and Don'ts. The book was given to all the division petty officers so all hands could use it. You knew just what you could do and what you couldn't do. If you were right, he would stand by you. If not, you'd had it.[21]

The ship's gunnery officer, Lieutenant Commander Peter Gaviglio, is also remembered as a strict taskmaster by Lieutenant (jg) Jerry Miller. Miller remembers one newly minted officer arriving on board the *Richmond* bursting with war-inspired patriotism: ". . . and he runs into Peter Gaviglio and the rules and regulations. It was very difficult for him to adjust to all this, but he made a valiant attempt." The new officer, Martin Dibner, would later write a memorable work of fiction drawn from his experiences on the *Richmond*.[22]

Captain Theodore Waldschmidt, the *Richmond*'s skipper, was a quiet man who is best remembered for his patience and seamanship. One of his men recalls that ". . . his appearance was what you would think a judge should have." Unfortunately, his relationship with Admiral McMorris was strained.

Not only did the ever critical admiral choose to find fault with Waldschmidt's performance, but the personalities of the two officers were diametrically opposed. McMorris did not hesitate to dress a subordinate down, while Waldschmidt preferred a quiet comment. McMorris was aggressively demanding, while Waldschmidt was quietly demanding and self-effacing. "It was obvious that he and McMorris were two different types of gentlemen," is the way Jerry Miller describes the situation. His strained relationship with the admiral was a burden that the *Richmond*'s captain bore privately.[23]

One of the *Richmond*'s sister ships was torpedoed and nearly sunk at Pearl Harbor. Another escaped from the Western Pacific in a fighting retreat. The remainder of the *Omaha* class were destined to serve the war out performing second-line duties. The *Richmond* was no exception. When war began, she was in South American waters, enforcing the neutrality zones proclaimed by President Roosevelt. She spent the first half of 1942 escorting convoys to the islands of Bora Bora and Tongatapu. War was not even distant thunder in those waters. There was no enemy but boredom and no combat. There *were* rats, as Jerry Miller relates:

> The first year in the South Pacific on those long convoys . . . it was not uncommon to go sixty days without a resupply. I remember one time on that cruiser getting a meal of beans and rice a couple of times a day. And that brought out the rats. They were down in the bottom of the holds. The rats were getting hungry, and we had a campaign on for a while against the rats. You'd be sitting in the wardroom, and the rats would run through on the overhead beams. We put up signs to block off the passageway—"detour"—and all that stuff. We had to put out an order for the crew to wear their shoes in their bunks at night, to sleep with their shoes on, because the rats would come in and nip them on the calluses of their feet. We had a good campaign on to kill rats. I think we had a fee of $1 a rat, or something like that, for the crew, and then, of course, the crew started raising rats to get the fees.[24]

The latter half of 1942 brought another tedious six months in South American waters. Sagging morale received a boost when the *Richmond* received orders to the North Pacific in December 1942.

No portent of a place in the history books was in the orders: the *Richmond* was going north to relieve one of her sister ships that had been weather damaged. After a short refit in Mare Island Navy Yard, she reported to Dutch Harbor in January 1943. Balmy weather and placid seas became only fond memories as the rigors of life in the Aleutians soon became evident to all hands. No one on board was affected in quite the same way as the ship's cooks, as described by Yeoman 2c Gene Purdy:

> One of their battles . . . was coping with the days on end of rough weather. All they could do was hang buckets of soup from the overhead and you . . . grabbed some when it swung by. Same for the coffee. They invented ways to keep the food on the stove so it would cook. However, we seemed to be able to blame every discomfort on the enemy and the war.[25]

Jerry Miller, who had been excited that the *Richmond* was at last going to a combat zone, learned that life in the Aleutians was not the escape from wearying routine that he had hoped:

> We had the long, dull periods . . . and the weather was very demoralizing up there. And we could never see any end to it. It all moved along so slow. You'd do a shore bombardment. And then, two months of nothing, just steaming and standing watches. We came into Adak occasionally, would drop the hook and sit there, but you could never really stop steaming, because any minute 80 knots of wind would come down and you'd start dragging the anchor, so you always had steam up for getting under way. You didn't get on a boat and go ashore. You sat there on the ship and waited till the next order came. Then, when under way again, you'd get your bucket and head for the foretop to stand your watch. We automatically got sick the first day out until we got adjusted to the roll and pitch again. Sitting up on the top of that big tripod mast never gave you a calm day. There was rarely a calm day in the Aleutians.[26]

Mess attendant 3c Gid Thomas,
Richmond.   Courtesy Gid Thomas

Yeoman Purdy, Jerry Miller, and their shipmates got to vent
a little of their discomfort on the enemy in mid-February when
the *Richmond* participated in the bombardment of Attu. The
ship was just to the south of the *Indianapolis* when the heavy
cruiser intercepted and sank the *Akagane Maru.* A month later,
the old light cruiser was headed for a fight that would more
than make up for the one she had missed.

Destroyers are the jacks-of-all-trades in every fleet and
the four tincans with McMorris were no exception. Two of
them, the *Dale* and the *Monaghan,* were of the *Farragut* class,

47

the first of the United States Navy's post–World War I destroyers. Not much bigger than one of the old four pipers, both ships commissioned in 1935. Both had been assigned to Destroyer Squadron 1 and spent all of their prewar careers in the Pacific. Both were among the ships enjoying a Sunday in Pearl Harbor. A measure of revenge was extracted by the *Monaghan* that morning when she sank one of the five Japanese midget subs lost that day.

Both ships were constantly on the move in the following months; the *Monaghan* was in the Battles of the Coral Sea and Midway, and did convoy duty in the South Pacific. She was sent to the Aleutians in the summer of 1942. In contrast to the feelings of anticipation the same orders would bring to the *Richmond*, no one aboard *Monaghan* was very excited. As one man puts it, "I'd say that no one was excited about being there while so much action was taking place in the South Pacific."[27] She no sooner got to the Aleutians than she was headed back to San Francisco. While participating in the abortive July attempt to bombard Kiska, she was rammed by another destroyer, necessitating a return to Mare Island for repairs.

Her stay in California was marked by the same skimming off of experienced men as happened to the *Salt Lake City*. One replacement draft was a batch of Texans who had been inspired to enlist en masse after hearing President Roosevelt deliver a patriotic speech. Rested, regunned, refitted, but not quite so experienced, the *Monaghan* headed north late in the summer. Like the cruisers, wartime additions had turned her into a crowded ship. There was some compensation for the overcrowding in that her supply officer was successful in preserving her prewar reputation as the best feeder in the Navy.[28]

Lieutenant Commander Peter Horn was the *Monaghan*'s second wartime skipper. He was an experienced destroyer officer, but because his predecessor was so well liked, he suffered somewhat in the eyes of the old hands. One of his sailors, Seaman 1c Ed Brown, has this to say about Horn:

I know that Captain Horn was not too well liked in general,

but I felt he was a fine officer. I stood my watches on the bridge so I had an opportunity to see him in action. He was a small man and resembled a cartoon character called "Alfred" that appeared in the *Saturday Evening Post* during those times. Captain Horn was an avid movie goer and was responsible for us getting movies on board. He never missed a show. Sometimes he would be a little late for the start of a movie so we would pound on a stanchion that ran from the mess hall up into the wardroom. We would call out, "Hey, Alfred, you're late," and he would come right down. I had numerous opportunities to speak with him but I only remember the first time as to what was said. Captain Horn had been getting on the signalmen because they were late in picking up light signals from other ships. I had been ribbing the signalmen for their plight when the Captain heard me. He asked me my name and then told me I had the job of picking up our call signal, which was "Fifty-four." Before he left I had become a pretty good signalman. Captain Horn was a fine seaman and no one could ever question his courage. He proved both [seamanship and courage] time and again during the *Monaghan*'s tour in the Aleutians.[29]

Another destroyer with an Irish name, the *Dale* had also been at Pearl Harbor. In the following months, she accompanied raids on New Guinea and Rabaul, did convoy duty throughout the South Pacific, served at Guadalcanal, and was screening the battleship *North Carolina* when that ship was torpedoed. She went to the Aleutians with her squadron mate.

Duty in the north afforded quite a contrast to these veterans of the South Pacific. Heat rash became a thing of the past as the cold and damp of the North Pacific penetrated every part of the ship. Sunshine during the morning watch was often replaced by howling wind and mountainous seas during the afternoon watch. The ships bucked and rolled wildly, and the men grew adept at eating while standing up. As liberty became only a memory, tempers often flared. Homemade fun had to take the place of the bars and nightspots of San Francisco and Honolulu. Out of nowhere, a rubber-band gun craze swept over the *Dale*. Sailors were soon staging mock ambushes and holdups all over the ship. Every man went about his duties

49

"armed," and rubber bands were at a premium. The ship's executive officer, Lieutenant Commander Ken Robinson, one day spied the jack o' the dust with a rubber-band gun Robinson describes as a "real beauty." He asked the man if he could borrow the gun just long enough to show it to the skipper, Commander Anthony Rorschach. The exec had not quite got all the way up the ladder leading to the bridge when he was spotted by his captain. With dismay in his voice, Rorschach cried out, "My God, you're not making them too?"[30]

As was customary in United States destroyers, the executive officer also doubled as navigator. Aleutian weather made it not the easiest of jobs. Star or sun sights were often few and far between. Charts were soon found to have some islands located as much as five miles out of their true positions. The single factor that made the navigation problem manageable was radar. Lieutenant Commander Hart Kait, exec and navigator of the *Monaghan* during her tenure in the Aleutians, writes, "I got to know the radar picture by heart and still have all the island tangents in mind."[31] Radar was indeed a boon to navigation, but skill at dead reckoning was also necessary; if there was no landmass within radar range, it was often the only way to determine ship's position.

The other two destroyers with McMorris, the *Bailey* and the *Coghlan*, were new ships of the *Benson*-class. Both were built by Bethlehem Steel—the *Bailey* at Staten Island and the *Coghlan* in San Francisco. First into commission was the *Bailey*, in May 1942. Her first skipper had the misfortune to ground her while on her shakedown cruise. He was relieved in command by Lieutenant Commander John Atkeson. Atkeson graduated from Annapolis in 1927 and subsequently did duty in both battleships and destroyers. He is said to have commanded with authority, was known as a fair man, was concerned for his men, but demanded discipline and loyalty in return. The first officer to report for duty to the *Bailey*'s pre-commissioning detail was Lieutenant (jg) Frank Ayers. He came to be very impressed with the new captain:

John Atkeson was an admirable captain. He was a fine ship handler and was loved by the officers and the crew. One of his trademarks was a cigar in his mouth seemingly from the time he arose in the morning until he hit his bunk at night. In a matter of months the ship became a cigar smoking ship in emulation of the skipper. Even the fuzz-faced recruits bought Red Dot cigars in the ship's store. It was a classic case of hero worship. Captain Atkeson was very soft spoken and modest. He was his own man. I remember an instance during a maneuver when the Commodore made it known that he thought the ship should go left. Captain Atkeson thought the opposite and without hesitation called for right standard rudder.[32]

Atkeson encountered no unexpected difficulties in wringing the new ship out and reported the *Bailey* ready for duty in August 1942. He was ordered to take her from Maine to New York Navy Yard, where the after mount of torpedo tubes was replaced by 40-mm antiaircraft guns. During the stay in New York, the *Bailey* became the flagship of Destroyer Squadron 14. The squadron commander, Captain Ralph Riggs, and his staff were embarked for only a short while before the *Bailey* left for the Aleutians.

During a layover in San Francisco, Ensign Harlan Bumpas joined the *Bailey* as her supply officer. The recent graduate of Supply School had originally been ordered to Pearl Harbor, but because his train was eighteen hours late in getting into San Francisco, he was reassigned to the just arrived *Bailey*. His introduction to the ship was hectic. When he reported on board, he was told that he had just twenty-four hours to draw the allotted amount of office equipment, arrange disbursing authority, and procure money to pay the crew. As the scheduled hour of departure fast approached, he found himself in San Francisco's Federal Reserve Bank counting $50,000 in cash. The Twelfth Naval District supply officer with him finally said, "If you expect to make that ship by three, son, you'd better throw the money in the bag and let's go." A Marine guard and a car were provided for him, and after a hectic ride across the city, he made the ship. He spent the next week in seasick misery as the *Bailey* battered her way northward. In late September 1942, when the ship arrived in Kodiak, Alaska, Bumpas immediately went ashore and bought himself five hamburgers and a quart of ice cream. He was grateful to at least have his feet on firm ground.[33]

The trip north was a foretaste of things to come. Gunner's Mate 3c Bob Walker describes the *Bailey*'s introduction to the rigors of life in the Aleutians.

> Weather! Bad, lousy, rough, rotten. Combine all these terms to describe the weather and then every once in a while it would really blow up a storm. The first forty-five days may have lulled everyone into thinking it wasn't too bad. Then it happened. We lost all . . . lifelines on the main deck from . . . the forecastle to the fantail. Depth charges had become wedged and canted in the racks, with some racks even partially torn loose. Even some of the 20-mm gun . . . supports were bent. Needless to say, only the basic essentials were remounted on the main deck. I think the farthest the *Bailey* ever rolled was 54° past vertical.[34]

Frank Ayers continues this bleak account:

> We had storm after storm. Rolls would be so severe we'd be thrown out of our bunks. We'd pile clothing and bedding under the mattress on the open side of our bunks to form a trough to sleep in. Stanchions had to be rigged at the wardroom table so we could lash our chairs to them and thereby stay at the table. One of our men was so chronically and deathly seasick he'd lie down in a passageway; men could step on him or stumble over him, it made no difference to him. The ship would pitch so deeply that our propellors would be more out of the water than in it. The seas were so severe that we lost a depth charge, portions of our rails and bulwarks, and topside gear such as potato lockers. Any man who served aboard destroyers in the Aleutians during the winter of 1942–1943 can truly say he's "been to sea."[35]

These severe conditions demanded extra protection for

the men with topside watch stations, but the authorized issue of foul weather gear was found to be insufficient. In compliance with his captain's orders, Bumpas was soon making the rounds of Kodiak, knocking on supply office doors. When an obdurate supply officer wouldn't provide the additional foul weather gear, Atkeson included Bumpas in the base commander's invitation to dinner. The obvious concern of Captain Atkeson for his men won the admiral's approval, and the necessary authorization was given to Bumpas to draw the extra gear. Bumpas found himself unpopular with the base supply officer but most impressed with his captain.[36]

Atkeson enjoyed a very good relationship with the squadron commander. When Commodore Riggs came on board, Atkeson offered to surrender his cabin, which was the largest available. The offer was declined by Riggs, who took a smaller cabin in its place. This gesture was the beginning of a professional and personal relationship with John Atkeson that would endure until Riggs's death. Lieutenant Commander George Peckham was Riggs's operations officer, a position that well qualifies him to offer this thumbnail sketch of the squadron commander:

> Captain Riggs was a soft-spoken, able and competent officer. I would consider him a very strong leader capable of making and carrying out hard and difficult decisions even under adverse conditions. All his destroyer captains and staff knew that he meant what he said and they had great confidence in his leadership.[37]

For physical exercise while at sea, the *Bailey*'s captain and the commodore walked twenty turns around the foc'sle, having determined that twenty turns equalled a mile. Since there wasn't enough room to walk abreast, captain and commodore paced off their laps single file.[38]

The last of the four Irish-named destroyers with McMorris, the *Coghlan*, commissioned in July 1942. Lieutenant (jg) John James was one of the officers who took part in the transformation of a group of stangers in Navy blue into what was to become a fighting crew:

> We commissioned the ship with a strong nucleus of experienced officers and men. The 180-odd boots and reserve ensigns we started with shaped up fast—you tend to shape up fast in wartime! Furthermore, there was much good spirit in the ship. Most of the boots were volunteers and wanted to have at the enemy. They learned fast because they wanted to. I can't think of a department, from Communications to Gunnery, that wasn't completely professional. The Commanding Officer, Commander Tompkins, was a great skipper. At first . . . I thought he was cold and austere. He was somewhat older than became the norm a little later on. He was a disciplinarian but no Captain Bligh. He expected performance and got it. He was somewhat aloof, as a CO has to be, was quiet spoken but could put iron in his voice if necessary. He knew his job completely and knew if you were doing yours.[39]

The *Coghlan* was also with the *Indianapolis* when the *Akagane Maru* was sunk. She was ordered to torpedo the hulk, but as was then common, the miserable American torpedoes failed to function. Her introduction was not auspicious, but the materiel failures of 18 February were soon to be forgotten.

The man in command of this assemblage of old and new ships, of green boots and battle-hardened veterans, was himself a battle-experienced officer. Rear Admiral Charles H. McMorris was an intense officer who had graduated from Annapolis fifth in the Class of 1912. His intelligence garnered him the nickname of "Soc," as he was reputed by his classmates to have the wisdom of Socrates. He rose steadily through the ranks of the prewar Navy, gaining a reputation as an excellent planner. He also commanded the destroyers *Shirk* and *Elliot*, taught English at Annapolis, and did a tour as navigator of the battleship *California*.

When war came, he was a staff officer in Hawaii, but soon found himself in command of the heavy cruiser *San Francisco*. He took her through the Cape Esperance fight, emerging

Vice Admiral Charles McMorris, *right*, shares a lighter moment
with Admiral Nimitz at Pearl Harbor.   National Archives

unscathed. Unknown to McMorris, it was ironic that on a
March day in 1943, he should be looking forward to being
joined by the *Salt Lake City*. In the Cape Esperance melee, the
San Francisco became separated from the other American ships.
As she rejoined the formation, tense lookouts in the *Salt Lake
City* saw her only as a darkened, unidentified ship closing on
their own. All four of the *Salt Lake City*'s turrets were quickly
brought to bear on the approaching ship. The main battery
control officer was poised to fire, needing only the word from
Captain Small. That officer fortunately held his fire, perhaps
suspecting the identity of the unknown ship. After repeated
queries, the *San Francisco* was identified, thus avoiding a point-
blank broadside from the *Salt Lake City*. Six months later, the
ship that almost ended McMorris's career was his main
strength.[40]

Soc McMorris was promoted to rear admiral after Cape

Esperance and went to the Aleutians in January 1943. He made the *Richmond* his flagship as soon as she reported for duty. Lieutenant Commander Al Ovrum and Lieutenant Ralph Millsap remember the admiral as an intense, feisty man. Millsap was impressed with the fact that McMorris arrived alongside the *Richmond* with only a single crate of records and the smallest of staffs. It was not too long afterward that Millsap got the very firm impression that Admiral McMorris was not one to tolerate mistakes. Millsap had the deck when the admiral called for a change of course. For some reason, the helmsman put the rudder over in the opposite direction. Although the helm was immediately reversed, the ship had not quite settled on the proper course when McMorris came storming into the pilothouse. Fixing his stern gaze on Millsap, he inquired if something had not been amiss in the execution of his order. "Yes, sir," was the reply. Not wanting to put the blame wholly on the helmsman, Millsap answered McMorris's inquiry about what had gone awry with an unintelligible mumble. With a curt, "Very well," McMorris departed. From that moment on, Millsap was determined that his performance before the admiral would be faultless.[41]

Al Ovrum had served under McMorris on board the *California*, so the admiral was no stranger to him. He describes McMorris as "hard-boiled" and a "tough nut" with those who chose not to work with him. He also remembers that McMorris had a sense of humor. As courtesy dictated and also to renew an old association, Ovrum called on McMorris after he embarked in the *Richmond*. After the pleasantries were exchanged, McMorris asked, "What's your job on here?" Ovrum replied, "I'm the navigator, Admiral." Recalling their former association aboard the *California*, the admiral laughed and said, "Oh God, I thought I'd get a good one." To which Ovrum could only reply, "Well, you taught me."[42]

A final example of McMorris's forthrightness is offered by Lieutenant Chuck Harrison, who was in charge of the *Richmond*'s after director. A young officer, new to the *Rich-*

mond, appeared on the bridge one day wearing a pair of woolen pants normally issued to enlisted men. This individual began immediately to explain that he was trying the pants out just to see how warm they were. According to Harrison, Mc-Morris's only comment was, "I don't give a goddamn if you pull a condom over your head and call it a raincoat."[43] Demanding, sharp-tongued, salty, Charles McMorris no doubt expected to see some combat when he got west of Attu. To his great surprise, the fight he was fated to find was much hotter than anticipated.

Aside from obvious differences in numbers, the only glaring disparity of strength between the ships of Task Group 16.6 and Fifth Fleet was that all the Japanese ships were armed with torpedoes. The American destroyers and the *Richmond* were so armed, but their weapons were puny in comparison to the Japanese Long Lance. It was in the spirit of the men that the American force was equal to the Japanese.

The prewar days of a small, elitist officer corps and a spit-and-polish Navy were gone forever. Those days had disappeared under a vast inrush of reservists, ninety-day wonders, and land-lubbers-made-sailors who hailed from every corner of the United States. As Ben Johnston of the *Salt Lake City* points out, when men are packed into a warship and spend many, many hours together at general quarters, pre-existing barriers of rank and social position tend to break down. There was little a man didn't come to know about his shipmate. What became important was whether a man carried his responsibilities or not. Gleaming brightwork and whites at Sea Detail became a thing of the past.

The Americans who flocked to the colors after Pearl Harbor had a single goal in mind—beat the hell out of the Japs and go home. The defeats of the early months imbued the Japanese with an aura of invincibility, but at Midway and especially at Guadalcanal, the men of the United States Navy showed a fighting spirit equal to the Japanese samurai. As proud as the Japanese were of their fighting spirit, in fact counting on it to overcome whatever materiel deficiencies they might face, this spirit was matched measure for measure by the United States Navy. The heady mixture of regular and reservist, career and hostilities-only sailor that was the World War II Navy, had a capacity for individual thought and action that the Japanese could not match.

Tradition and culture dictated that the great mass of Japanese servicemen were oriented toward unquestioning obedience to higher authority. Every Japanese serviceman was burdened with written and unwritten, traditional rules that covered every aspect of his life. It was a weight that tended to cause a noticeable fixity of purpose in Japanese military operations. Defeat was inadmissible, and even the appearance of defeat dictated but one course: death at one's own hand. The cultural differences between the Imperial Navy and the United States Navy were therefore quite vast. United States Navy regulations told a man what he could not do; everything else was permissible. A kind of high-spirited rowdiness is inherent in the American national character. It is balanced by the feeling that common sense is also important. Naval discipline harnessed those traits just enough to focus the energy of a generation to the business at hand. The teamwork necessary to fight a dedicated, skillful enemy was built, but not at the expense of common-sense initiative. The ability of American fighting men to think for themselves retrieved more than one victory from defeat during the long course of World War II. On 26 March 1943, it was a characteristic that saved the lives of several hundred American sailors and the career, if not the life, of one American admiral.

TG 16.6 Continues to the West

By 24 March, unsettled seas had become a full-fledged storm. The low-slung *Salt Lake City* began to suffer the fury of the North Pacific. Her starboard catapult and other topside fittings were damaged and her forward life rafts carried away.

The height of the storm came during the midwatch of 24 March. George O'Connell had that watch, an experience he describes in detail. He begins with a description of the clothing he had to don for a watch topside:

> I put on long-handled underwear, jungle-cloth clothing, an aviation arctic suit [which consisted] of a zippered, fur-lined jacket, a pair of high-suspendered, fur-lined leather trousers which zippered up the sides, a pair of fur-lined leather flight boots, and a fur-lined leather helmet. Over all this, I wore a waterproofed, canvas foul weather parka suit. Heaven help anyone so clothed who might lose his footing, because he would probably require someone else to help him get back to his feet.

Making his way to the bridge with some difficulty, he relieved the watch:

> The midwatch of March 24 was one to remember. At about 0200 . . . McMorris ordered the task group to change course and speed. We went from the trough directly into the sea. To describe the *Salt Lake City* as a cork on an angry sea would be incorrect. Under the impetus of its engines, the *Salt Lake City* would comb one wave, bow tilted upward . . . until the bow was completely out of the water. Like an enormous lever, the bow would fall abruptly downward, and the fantail would shoot upward, propellors spinning. Still . . . driving inexorably onward, the *Salt Lake City* would literally dive into the base of the next wave. Tons of water would come crashing down onto the forecastle, sweeping over Turrets I and II and . . . the open bridge. Shortly after our turn into the sea, and after only a few moments of that dangerous agony . . . Commander Bitler came to the bridge. Visibly disturbed, he said the ship patently could not take the punishment. With the Captain's permission the following message was sent to . . . McMorris: "Advise slowing to ten knots to avoid excessive pounding." The OTC immediately signaled "Speed 10" and the pounding diminished. Repair parties then inspected the ship. Some plates were found stove in, some stanchions were bent, one store room was flooded, one vent intake topside was carried away allowing the entrance

of water. However, the damage was judged manageable, which was heartening. My watch was over at 0400 and the ship's agony had subsided.[44]

The fury of the storm also drove the ship's warrant officers from their berthing compartment in the forward part of the hull. The impetus of the pounding sea was causing the longitudinal bulkhead forming one boundary of their compartment to flex and pop like a giant toy cricket. The noise was too much; everyone fled the compartment for quieter spaces. Ben Johnston had been on board the *Salt Lake City* for four years, but had never experienced a storm like this one. So agonizingly slow and steep were the ship's rolls that he says, "There were times when I was in fear of my life."[45] The wartime accumulation of topweight caused the ship to pause, linger at the extreme arc of the roll, and then, ever so slowly, start back. It was a frightening experience for all hands in the *Salt Lake City*. Even though bad weather was old news to the destroyermen, Ed Brown's diary records the weather damage suffered by the *Monaghan*.[46]

A most undesirable effect of the heavy weather was that it interfered with the *Salt Lake City*'s intensive training program. In an effort to regain the fine edge of readiness she enjoyed before the layup in Pearl Harbor, a program of extra general quarters drill had been instituted. All the standard control, gunnery, and ammo-handling procedures were covered, as well as every conceivable casualty. The escorting destroyers were used as drill targets, providing valuable experience in tracking and ranging on another ship. The drill hours were added to the normal sunrise and sunset general quarters. It meant that the *Salt Lake City*'s crew spent several hours of every day at their battle stations.

There were many drills outside of general quarters as well. Officers and enlisted lookouts alike spent hours studying recognition materials. One exercise involved the rapid flashing of ship and aircraft silhouettes on a movie screen, the watchers being required to correctly identify each silhouette. Unfortunately, the heavy seas of 23–24 March caused most of the extra drills to be canceled.

In typical Aleutian fashion, mid-morning on the 25th found the seas calm enough for the *Salt Lake City* to refuel the *Bailey* and the *Coghlan*. First in line was the *Bailey*. As the line-handling parties huddled against the piercing cold and freezing spray, John Atkeson took his ship alongside the heavy cruiser. In her role as oiler-cum stores ship, the *Salt Lake City* pumped 1,340 barrels of fuel oil to her consort and delivered 200 pounds of bread, 300 pounds of sugar, 60 dozen eggs, 1,152 candy bars, and 30 precious gallons of ice cream. The emulation of Atkeson by the *Bailey*'s crew is plainly evident in the fact that 2,500 cigars are also listed among the stores transferred to the destroyer. The *Coghlan* was next at the pump, and although she received a like amount of stores, there are no cigars listed in the record of transfer. The *Richmond* took lifeguard station 1,000 yards astern while fueling was in progress. Plans were made to fuel the *Dale* and the *Monaghan* on the 28th, but subsequent events intervened.

Captain Rodgers's deck force was still wrestling with the heavy fueling hoses when Admiral McMorris received a message from task force headquarters. According to McMorris's account, he was advised to continue the patrol at his discretion. Soon thereafter, another message from Adak erased any thoughts of an early return. Admiral Kinkaid had been warned by Pearl Harbor's codebreakers that the Japanese were at sea and were likely to be in the area. Communications intelligence was about to precipitate a battle unique to the Pacific war.

At 1600, 25 March, McMorris ordered his force to assume a scouting line. The ships took stations six miles apart, forming a line thirty miles long. McMorris had several reasons for his choice of disposition: he cited the varying radar capabilities of his ships and the ever-present concern with the weather. The most important consideration, as circumstances would show, was the need for rapid concentration of the task group. The American ships spent the night of 25–26 March steaming athwart a line between the Japanese bases in the Kuriles and Attu. As if in preparation for the coming test, the bad weather of the previous days continued to abate throughout the night. The thread of chance that weaves through so much of the fabric of war was slowly and inexorably drawing several thousand Japanese and American sailors toward a deadly meeting. A battle in the Aleutians could not change the course of the war; to those involved, however, the next few hours would be of life or death importance.

CHAPTER 2

Contact!
0730–0830 26 March 1943

At 0730 on the morning of Friday, 26 March 1943, the *Richmond* was in position 168° – 32′E, 53° – 16′N. Paramushiro was about 500 miles to the southwest and Adak about 500 miles to the east. The American task group was in the same scouting disposition taken up the previous afternoon. The ships were on course 020°T, making turns for 15 knots, and zig-zagging to Plan Eight. They were aligned on an axis of 350°– 170° in the following order: the *Coghlan*, *Richmond*, *Bailey*, *Dale*, *Salt Lake City*, and *Monaghan*. The sky was heavily overcast, ceiling a low 4–5,000 feet; in dramatic contrast to the past few days, visibility was thirteen to nineteen miles with a slight morning haze. The wind was from the southeast at 8 knots, the air temperature was a frigid 30–35°F, the cold, grey sea was calm with no swells, and the barometer was holding steady at 30.33″ Hg. Standard wartime practice in the U.S. Navy was for ships to go to routine general quarters one hour before sunrise. Among the ships of Task Group 16.6, the *Dale* had already manned dawn GQ stations, and the others were in

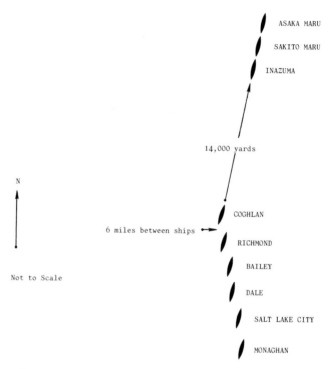

Figure 1. Contact! 0730—26 March 1943; TG 16.6 meets Fifth Fleet.

the process of, or about to do so. Scuttlebutt about the possibility of a fight was rampant, but there was little else to distinguish that Friday morning from a hundred other wartime mornings.

The familiar tedium of morning routine was broken as the hands of the clock swept by 0730. Three unidentified surface contacts made their luminescent appearance on the *Coghlan*'s radar screen. Her officer of the deck did not hesitate; he quickly picked up the TBS (radio-telephone) handset and reported the contacts to the flagship. Two contacts were also showing on the *Richmond*'s radar, and more began to crop up immediately. The alert was passed down the line with a decided economy of words: "We have three to five targets on the SG." The flagship didn't have to say anything else. The unseen ships could only be Japanese. In the single sweep of a radar, daily drill became the real thing.

A messenger alerted Ralph Millsap. "We have three targets on the SG. When we go to GQ, it will be a business general quarters." Lieutenant Commander Leonard Branneman, the *Richmond*'s executive officer, was just leaving the wardroom when the GQ alarm went off. He turned to McMorris's flag lieutenant and remarked, "This sounds like something cooking." A laconic "Could be," was the only reply. Morning general quarters was facetiously known as Sunrise Serenade in the *Bailey*, where the gas alarm was used to signify routine GQ. It had no sooner died away than the general alarm, sounded by John Atkeson himself, rang through the ship. Harlan Bumpas was still hurrying into his clothes when the general alarm sounded. Men rushing to the forward magazines and handling rooms were passing his stateroom. With each inquiry he made, the purported total of enemy ships rose. By the time he reached his battle station in the Coding Room, the supposed total of enemy ships had reached outlandish proportions.[47] In the *Salt Lake City*, Bob Taplett had the gunnery watch in the foretop:

> I can still recall the exhilaration of the masts of those ships beginning to appear hull down on the horizon and ordering the main battery to train on the enemy and to be prepared to fire on order. I thought to myself at the time, "I'll bet this is the first time a Marine officer was going to take enemy ships under fire from the main battery of a heavy cruiser." Alas, the rapid closing of the range was changed . . . and the sounding of General Quarters brought the ship's Gunnery Officer to his battle station.[48]

So it went. The usual drowsy languor was shattered, and the pace of every man quickened as the rumor and anticipation of the previous days was replaced by the knowledge that the

65

enemy had been encountered. Throughout the American ships, hatches and watertight doors were slammed shut and dogged down. On went steel helmets and headsets. With practiced ease, the veterans slid into their seats at the telescopes, took up their positions at the throttles, and prepared to start powder and shells up to the guns. Nervous newcomers eyed the veterans and tried hard to remember what they had so recently been taught. No one is exempt from general quarters, so a Marine turned the *Salt Lake City's* lone prisoner out of the brig and sent him hurrying to his battle station. In a matter of minutes, the last manned-and-ready report was received by the various control stations. Via TBS, McMorris ordered the task group to concentrate on the *Richmond*. All ships were ordered to immediately bring all boilers on the line in anticipation of the need for all possible speed.*

A well-clad Jerry Miller, who was the *Richmond's* forward control officer, was in his battle station in the windowless foretop. After a quick study through his binoculars, he reported five enemy ships, their numbers more a dim suggestion than clearly seen. Radar and visual contacts did not yet jibe, as the *Coghlan* was reporting five radar contacts and the *Richmond* only three. One of the Japanese captains must have still been unsure that the strangers were Americans, because several challenges were made by flashing light. The Americans

---

*It was customary for cruising ships to rotate the number of boilers on the line. Four boilers will obviously consume less fuel than eight, thereby extending endurance of the ship. The problem with cold boilers is that they must be fired gradually, allowing time for all components to expand with the heat. Also, a boiler must be hot enough to produce steam before the lines to the turbines can be cut in. A slug of water to a turbine will wreck it in short order. By the skill of their engineers, and with some luck, all the American ships except the *Monaghan* were able to bring their cold boilers up to operating temperature without damage.

In his account of this battle, Samuel Eliot Morison takes the Japanese to task for not having all their boilers on the line. Since the records clearly show the same situation to apply to the American ships, his chiding of the Japanese is chauvinistic nonsense.[49]

had a more lethal kind of reply in mind, so the challenges were ignored. McMorris recorded a first impression of having run into one or two merchantmen escorted by one or two destroyers and a light cruiser. At 0740, the *Richmond*'s CIC reported the enemy course to be 080°, speed 13 knots, range 21,000 yards. The slim bow of the flagship began to swing around to the right as course was altered to parallel that of the enemy. A host of coincidental departures, changes of speed, speeds of advance, vagaries of weather, and a not so coincidental knowledge of the enemy's intentions had coalesced into a contact. The American task group had intercepted Fifth Fleet as it reached the southern end of its waiting line.

By 0745, the *Bailey* and the *Coghlan* had taken stations 3,000 yards off the port bow of the flagship. McMorris set the TBS circuit acrackle as he ordered the *Salt Lake City* and the other two destroyers to expedite closing up. What was apparently a group of lightly screened transports was still being counted when it turned to the northwest and began to open the range. McMorris was anxious to turn after them, but prudence dictated that he wait for the *Salt Lake City* to join the *Richmond*. Range to the enemy ships had increased to 27,000 yards by 0800, so McMorris once again ordered course changed to parallel the Japanese. It takes even a speedy destroyer more than a few minutes to close a twenty-four-mile gap: the *Dale*, *Salt Lake City*, and *Monaghan* were coming as hard as they could, but still trailed far behind the flagship. McMorris had no option but to control his impatience, try to keep the enemy in sight, and wait.

Even though the enemy had been in sight for nearly thirty minutes, the Americans were still unsure about the exact strength or disposition of his force. The wink of signal lights could be seen, but the smoke created by cold boilers being lighted off, the predawn haze, and the mixing of silhouettes as the Japanese ships changed formation, combined to defeat accurate observation. Many pairs of binoculars were trained on the distant ships. Yet by 0811, the *Richmond* had incorrectly reported one large merchantman, one single-stack destroyer, and three small merchantmen to McMorris. At 0815, she reported yet another destroyer. McMorris still thought he possessed a favorable disparity of strength and later recorded that ". . . a Roman holiday was in prospect." Captain Rodgers thought it looked like ". . . an easy day's pickings."[50]

In both American cruisers, those who could see the enemy ships envisioned a walkover. Ralph Millsap was on the bridge with McMorris and remembers that the admiral was almost literally hopping up and down in his anticipation of getting among the transports. Worthy Bitler had the feeling that the Japanese were "duck soup." Howard Grahn likened the heavy cruiser to ". . . the fox in the chicken coop." At his battle station in Turret II, Ben Johnston heard someone say over the phone circuit, "It looks like a field day because it's only a couple of fat merchant ships." The word of an apparently impending slaughter was cheerfully passed from station to station in all six American ships. Some of the men in the *Dale* and the *Monaghan* were even afraid that the action would be over before they could get to the scene. It didn't look to be much of a fight, but to Yeoman 1c Chuck Vasey, it looked *too* easy. He thought it had to be some kind of a trap. At 0817, a plain language contact report was radioed off:

> COMCRUDIV 1 TO CTF 16 CONTACT GROUP OF SHIPS EASTERLY COURSE LAT 53-00 LONG 168-40 X CCD1 SENDS TO TF CMDR X CONCENTRATING TO ATTACK

One staff officer at Adak, Lieutenant Commander Walter Jenkins, recalls that the contact report was occasion for ". . . gratification, suspense, joy, anxious moments, great satisfaction, and at the same time, plans for repairs and ammunition replenishment."[51]

What still appeared to be a milling group of transports and light combatants was now slightly off the *Richmond*'s port bow. Admiral McMorris, Captain Rodgers, and all hands soon got a nasty shock. By 0824, the *Richmond*'s radar indicated the presence of four more ships, bringing the total present to ten. The men in the foretop of both the *Richmond* and the *Salt Lake City* swung their binoculars to the right in response to these new radar contacts. It took only minutes for them to see an ominous sight rising over the horizon. To the consternation of all, what was appearing were not the masts of more merchantmen, but the fighting tops of heavy cruisers.

A report from the forward director started the bad news down the wire in the *Salt Lake City*: "Two heavy cruisers, one, maybe two light cruisers, and six destroyers, hull down, range 40,000 yards, high speed. Target angle zero two zero, moving to intervene between the *Richmond* and the transports." The many long hours spent poring over grainy photos in *Jane's*, memorizing official recognition manuals, and compiling homemade charts were put to use as men sought to identify these new enemies. George O'Connell listened intently to the information flowing into his headset, and then phoned the bridge:

> Conn, Control. We have in sight cover force. Two heavy cruisers, two light cruisers, and six destroyers, hull down, distance 38,000 yards, bearing forty degrees on the starboard bow at high speed, target angle zero two zero degrees, apparently attempting to get between the transports and the *Richmond*. Leading heavy cruiser identified as *Nachi*, second heavy cruiser *Atago*-class. Light cruisers are *Natori* class. Director One is on the leading heavy cruiser. All turrets are matching.[52]

As the enemy ships rose into sight, it could be seen from the spotting top that their turrets were already bearing. The totally unexpected appearance of the enemy heavy cruisers is reported to have caused the *Coghlan*'s gunnery officer to excitedly call down from the director, "Jesus Christ, there's two battleships out there and they ain't canoes." This and other identifications were wrong, but the fact that the situation had radically and unfavorably changed was unmistakable. To make matters worse, the Japanese heavy units were obviously be-

69

tween the Americans and any dash toward the airbases to the east. The news gave Howard Grahn the terrible feeling that ". . . the chickens had all turned to wolves and the door was locked." Grahn was one of those people who relieved tension by chewing gum. Since gum was a scarce item, one wad had to do duty many times over. As he sat in the after director watching the enemy ships continue their steady march over the horizon, Grahn reached for his well-used but still serviceable wad of gum. The *Salt Lake City* "family" let him down on this occasion; the gum was gone from its hiding place. To Jerry Miller, the unexpected appearance of the *Nachi* and the *Maya* meant that ". . . we were going to have a very interesting day." Captain Rodgers summed up the new situation rather succinctly when he said to Worthy Bitler, "Worthy, I think we've got a bull by the tail."[53]

By sunrise, McMorris knew he was faced by two heavy cruisers, two light cruisers, and four destroyers. No one can know, of course, but his surprise must have been profound. The ability of Naval Intelligence to keep track of Japanese naval movements meant that the ships were assigned to the North Pacific in direct balance to the Fifth Fleet. McMorris left Dutch Harbor secure in the knowledge that he might meet lightly screened transports or, at best, a force no stronger than his own. Instead, he found himself faced by two heavy cruisers, both faster and better protected than his single ship. McMorris's flagship had heavier guns than the Japanese light cruisers, but there were two of them. A supposed easy day's pickings had gone aglimmering in the space of a few minutes.

At 0830 on that Friday morning so many years ago, the responsibility for life or death decisions that military commanders accept must have lain heavily on Charles McMorris's shoulders. He was charged with preventing the Japanese from supplying Attu or Kiska, but his orders also directed him to avoid engaging superior enemy forces. All the training and preparation of a naval lifetime was called into play. The right decision could possibly bring defeat to his country's enemy

70

and honor to his service. The wrong decision could very well bring death to several thousand of his men. Nor did he have long to make a decision; the Japanese would be within firing range in only minutes. McMorris recorded a variety of alternatives which he said came to his mind: "There was a chance, recognizedly remote, that by turning toward the auxiliaries they might be brought under gun fire . . . in any event an initial movement toward the enemy auxiliaries appeared to offer the most favorable opportunity to the enemy for him to make mistakes." McMorris also thought there was a chance that the Japanese commander might try to send the transports on to Attu, thereby exposing them to air attack. He did note, "It would be important, of course, not to be drawn in to a killing range against the superior force."[54]

Ralph Millsap feels that the admiral had only one course open to him: "In his battle report, McMorris has himself carefully weighing alternatives . . . but really, there wasn't a hell of a lot for him to do except for what he actually did." Jerry Miller is of the same opinion: "I think the reason he [McMorris] took the course he did was there was no other alternative. If he'd headed to the east, he'd have gotten blown up!" In Millsap's opinion, McMorris had less than five minutes to decide upon his course of action.[55] At 0833, McMorris ordered course 330°, but did not yet increase speed. The *Dale* had joined the *Monaghan* astern of the *Salt Lake City*, but all three ships were still some 5,000 yards astern of the *Richmond*.

The preliminaries were now over. Task Group 16.6 and Fifth Fleet were about to put each other to the extreme test. For a few men on both sides, it was to be their last day. For an era of surface naval warfare, it was to be the last battle.

THE BATTLE OF THE KOMANDORSKI ISLANDS:
0830–1005

At 0830, Admiral Hosogaya ordered speed increased to 25 knots. His ships were now in two columns; the *Nachi* led one, followed immediately astern by the *Maya* and the *Tama*.

71

All four destroyers were in column astern of the *Abukuma*, which trailed the *Tama* on her starboard quarter. At 0840, the *Nachi* and the *Maya* opened fire on the *Richmond* at a range of 21,000 yards. The first salvo put a finish to the efforts of the *Nachi*'s aviation detachment to launch the Pete aircraft on her starboard catapult. Muzzle blast from the after four guns smashed the plane beyond repair. A fire hazard, the wrecked plane was pushed over the side. Later in the day, the upturned float of this plane was sighted by an American search plane, leading to the mistaken impression that the American ships had shot a spotting plane down. American action reports also credit one of the Japanese light cruisers with launching a plane, but this is inaccurate. Neither the *Tama* nor the *Abukuma* had aircraft embarked on this occasion.[56]

The first enemy salvo was correct in deflection, but 1,000 yards short of the *Richmond*. The second was a straddle. Leonard Branneman was at his battle station in the *Richmond*'s secondary conn, a position from which he witnessed the arrival of these opening salvos:

> From my battle station I happened to be looking over the side of the ship and saw *most* [Branneman's emphasis] clearly the salvo land . . . short of our starboard side, just exactly abreast of where I stood. [It] looked like ducks diving into the water. Their second salvo passed directly over our ship, cutting an antenna on the way over. At that point, I thought of *our* spotting procedure—short—over—ON.[57]

These salvos shook the *Richmond* so severely that down in Radio Central, Ralph Millsap turned to his leading radioman and said, "That's a hit. That's a hit!" Coxswain Turner thought, "Mare Island, here we come."[58] Damage control parties were dispatched to look for damage, but found none.

The first two Japanese salvos were a graphic demonstration of things to come. Fortunately for the *Richmond*, Hosogaya's flagship was almost immediately beset by a severe engineering casualty. As in the American ships, the *Nachi* had

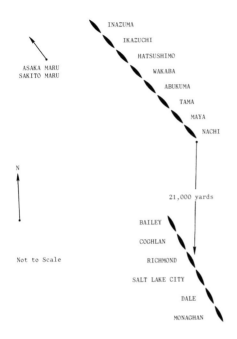

Figure 2. 0840—26 March 1943; *Nachi* opens fire on *Richmond*.

been steaming on an economical combination of boilers. The cold boilers were being forced as fast as possible, but not all were up to operating pressure when the *Nachi* opened fire. The generators supplying electrical power to the guns were inadvertently cut into a boiler with insufficient pressure, causing a complete loss of power to the turrets. The rhythm of the *Nachi*'s control and main battery personnel was broken while her engineers struggled to restore the electrical load. It was only a slight respite, but it stayed at least a couple of salvos that might have fallen on the *Richmond*.

At the same moment that the Japanese opened fire, McMorris ordered speed increased to 25 knots. The task group was concentrated at last, forming a relatively compact for-

73

mation some 5,200 yards long. From his perch high in the *Salt Lake City*'s foretop, George O'Connell was putting the finishing touches on the prefiring ritual. Speaking in the monotonic argot of the gunner's world, he told his acolytes in the directors and turrets, "All stations, Control. Director fire collective, Director One controlling, Spot One spot, shoot on three ready lights." He then called the bridge and said, "Conn, Control. Primers will not, repeat, not be loaded until your order, but we will load all guns except for primers." And to the turrets, "All turrets, Control. Except for primers, all guns load." Four turret Ready lights flashed on. O'Connell again called the bridge, "Conn, Control. Except for primers, all guns are loaded and ready."[59] A similar ritual was taking place in the *Richmond*. The guns were now loaded, pointed, ready. Only a few more words of the firing litany needed to be spoken.

The naval gunner is dealing with a complex problem. He is shooting from a platform that is moving about three axes at a target doing the same. He must take into consideration such diverse things as his own speed, speed of the target, powder and gun temperatures, the wind's effect on the flight of the shell, the rotation of the earth while the shell is in flight, and many other factors. All the necessary ballistic data had long since been fed into the gunfire computers by the time Japanese shells began to crash around the *Richmond*. Still no order to open fire came from the flagship. Insistent queries began to be heard on the *Salt Lake City*'s gunnery circuit. One voice even suggested that Captain Rodgers should open fire and take the consequences later. George O'Connell was growing fretful because he knew very well that the *Salt Lake City* was not built for a close-range slugging match, especially against two opponents.

Because the most important bulwark of the Navy is discipline, no gun could shoot until Admiral McMorris gave the order. The Americans endured Fifth Fleet's fire for a long two minutes. At 0842, somewhat belatedly to Japanese eyes, the order to commence firing was given. O'Connell passed the word to his men: "All stations, Control. Load primers. Commence firing, commence firing." Tongues of flame leapt from the gun muzzles as the *Richmond* and the *Salt Lake City* let fly at their tormentors. James Turner was pointer on the *Richmond*'s Number Seven gun. He later recorded the opening moments of the battle:

> "Match pointers in train and elevation. Prime." At that time I could see several ships on the horizon. I saw a flash from two ships followed by another flash. "Commence firing! Commence firing!" the gun captain yelled. I looked up from my instruments once to see what was going on. Five shots landed short about fifty yards in front of my sight port followed by five more in the same place. I could not see where our shots were landing.[60]

A closing rate of over 50 knots soon brought the *Bailey* and the *Coghlan* into gun range. The piercing crack of their 5-inch guns began to contribute to the sounds of battle enveloping the task group. Their fifty-four-pound shells were not capable of piercing the armor of either the *Nachi* or the *Maya*, but they could wreak havoc on the exposed upper works and they could hurt the light cruisers. They both initially concentrated their fire on the *Nachi*. The *Maya*, meanwhile, had shifted her attention from the *Richmond* to the *Salt Lake City*. The thunderclap arrival of her first salvo around the latter ship signaled to Rodgers and his men that they had taken a very much unwanted position on center stage.

Via TBS, McMorris ordered both of his cruisers to launch their aircraft. Having planes aloft to spot fall of shot would greatly aid the gunners. A quick "Understood" came back from the *Salt Lake City*. Before any action could be taken, McMorris exempted the *Richmond* from his order. The order still stood to the *Salt Lake City*, but would not be carried out. Damage control doctrine dictated that the planes were normally left unfueled and the gasoline supply piping drained, thereby minimizing the fire hazard. Normal practice was to run the aircraft engines at routine morning GQ, using just enough fuel to warm them up. When contact with the enemy was first announced, both aircraft were sitting on their catapults, unfueled. (The starboard catapult had been storm damaged and was inoperable.) Secure in the knowledge provided by *Ultra*, McMorris felt no need to order the planes aloft. The dramatic, and unexpected, appearance of the Japanese heavy cruisers created a pressing need for the planes. Unfortunately, the order to launch came almost simultaneously with the order to open fire. The same precautions that normally kept the planes unfueled also stipulated that no fueling was to be done once the ship had opened fire. Rodgers also knew very well that to expose a fuel-laden aircraft to the steady fall of enemy shellfire was to court disaster. Another factor that may have influenced Rodgers was the following wind. His ship's catapults were fairly low to the water, a fact that required the best possible relative wind for a successful launch. Whatever the reason, the *Salt Lake City*'s planes remained on board.[61]

The same reasons may explain McMorris's cancellation of the launching order issued to the *Richmond*. It has also been surmised that McMorris may have feared being unable to recover the planes once they were launched. None of these reasons explain his after-battle comment that he felt he might have a more pressing need of the planes later. It is hard to imagine a more pressing need than he had at the moment. The flagship's senior aviator was seen pleading with the admiral for a launch as forcefully as permitted a junior officer. It was not to be; the *Richmond*'s planes also remained on their catapults.[62]

McMorris may also have been distracted by the volume of gunfire being directed at his ships. His task group and the Japanese were engaged in a furious exchange that was roiling the water with many shell splashes. Salvo after salvo from the *Tama* was straddling the *Richmond*, shaking her severely but scoring no hits. The *Bailey* shifted her fire to the *Tama* in an effort to take the heat off the flagship, but enemy shells continued to pour in. A mile astern of the *Richmond*, Jim Brewer's gunners were hard at work. George O'Connell writes:

> Director I and Control Forward were as silent as a tomb, except for the background music of the soft, even modulated, monotone announcements of range and bearing, and the more authoritative foreground music of the announcements of the pointer: "Fire One." The turrets belched simultaneously. The foretop cracked like a buggy whip. "Fire Two." Again the turrets belched. Again the tops whipped. "Fire Three." Again the familiar whip in the tops. Salvo intervals were an unbelievable 16 seconds; twice as fast as the *Nachi*, and perhaps four times as fast as the *Atago*. The tempo of announcements and reports, and the interval between salvos was the only clue to the pent-up excitement in the ship. We now had three salvos in the air, . . . with a programmed ladder: Salvo One with its cold gun corrections; Salvo Two with a down 300; Salvo Three with an up 600. All was proceeding smoothly. A very good drill. [63]

Three minutes after the Americans opened fire, McMorris ordered a 40° turn to port, away from the oncoming enemy. He wrote, "Both sides were shooting well, but the odds were too great against us to continue. It seemed expedient to retire." [64]

Led by the *Bailey*, the American ships began to swing away to a southwesterly heading. One by one, the forward gun mounts began to fall silent as the direction of the turn blocked them out. As the *Richmond* completed the turn, only her after turret could bear, and control of the guns had to be switched to the after director. Ben Johnston and his men got an unwanted respite when the turn brought the *Salt Lake City*'s Number II turret up against the limit stops. Japanese interpretation of the turn was unequivocal; the Americans were fleeing. In an attempt to slow or stop them, eight huge Long Lance torpedoes blasted away from the *Nachi*'s starboard tubes. It would take several minutes for the accuracy of the shot to be known. In the meantime, oft-drilled torpedomen began

nov 1943

Gunner's Mate 1c Ray Amdahl, No. II turret,
Salt Lake City.   Courtesy Ray Amdahl

sweating eight more of the 6,000-pound monsters into the tubes.

The voices of the time of flight clock operator and the spotting officer had meanwhile joined the chorus of battle being heard over the *Salt Lake City*'s gunnery circuit. "Splash One" from the clock operator told the spotting officer that the first salvo was about to land. Peering through his long-base stereo rangefinder, the spotting officer watched the blue-tinged splashes raised by the *Salt Lake City*'s plunging shells erupt around the *Nachi*. "No change, no change." The firing solution was good. "Splash Two." "No change, no change." "Splash Three." "Straddle, hit, no change." Two armor-piercing shells from her third salvo hit the Japanese flagship. One hit the after starboard corner of the bridge, killing several signalmen and severing the electrical leads between the main battery director and the turrets. A gout of flame was seen to shoot up, followed by billows of smoke. A fire was started, but was quickly controlled. Admiral Hosogaya's staff was arrayed in the vicinity of the hit, but miraculously the blast and shrapnel spared all of them. The second shell severed the starboard after leg of the mainmast. Two minutes later, another 8-inch shell tore into the *Nachi*. It destroyed her starboard catapult, damaged her torpedo compartment, killed two men, and wounded several others. Rodgers's men were shooting very well. They fired twenty salvos at the *Nachi*, scoring three hits and eight straddles before shifting to the *Maya*. From the American point of view, it is possible that the first hit was the most important of the battle.

In the after-battle recollections of both sides, there is some controversy attendant to these hits. Samuel Eliot Morison asserts that they had to come from the *Salt Lake City* because the *Richmond* was not firing. He is in error. The various logs kept during the battle clearly show that the *Richmond* opened fire at 0842 and ceased fire at 0903, eighteen minutes after the *Nachi* was hit. Opinion is not evidence, but several of the *Salt Lake City*'s officers are certain their ship scored the hits. Jim Brewer is convinced that the time of flight of the opening salvos is too coincident with the hit to allow for any other explanation. He recalls that as the flame shot up from the *Nachi*'s superstructure, he turned to Captain Rodgers and said, "Captain, we've got him! Let's barrel in and finish him off!" Bob Matusek was peering through his turret periscope when the *Nachi* was hit: "I happened to have the *Nachi* in my periscope at the time she was hit. No doubt in my mind that we hit her. Sure was a pretty sight. The smoke just boiled out

79

from around the bridge area!" The *Coghlan's* director officer reported two hits on the *Nachi* at 0845 and recorded that they appeared to come from the *Salt Lake City*. A like statement is found in the *Monaghan's* Action Report: "One salvo from the *Salt Lake City* was observed to hit the leading heavy cruiser . . . just forward of the bridge structure early in the engagement."[65]

One who feels very differently is Ralph Millsap. He is a forceful, articulate man who is obviously very proud of his service in the *Richmond*. It is his opinion that his ship scored the first blows struck by the Americans: "There is no question; I believe that the *Richmond* scored the hits on the *Nachi* which almost . . . halved the enemy's firepower and really brought us down on an even term with the Japanese." He bases his opinion on a post-battle discussion with another officer, post-war interrogations of Japanese witnesses, the official Japanese account of the battle, and the fact that the *Nachi* was hit with two shells. Millsap's former shipmate, Jerry Miller, disagrees: "I don't think there's any chance at all that the *Richmond* hit the *Nachi* in the initial exchange of gunfire. The ranges were always way out at the extreme for the *Richmond*." As forward control officer, Miller directed most of the *Richmond's* fire during the battle.[66]

Millsap feels that the testimony of Kintaro Miura is particularly important. Commander Miura categorically stated that the major hits on the *Nachi* were all 15 cm (6-inch) hits. However, Miura also testified that it was a 5-inch shell that started the fire on the *Nachi's* bridge. None of the American destroyers claimed such a hit. In addition, Miura testified that the *Nachi* received five 6-inch hits in the initial exchange. Only two hits are mentioned in the *Nachi's* Action Report and only three hits are listed in the Japanese historical account of the battle. Another officer who was on the *Nachi's* bridge had differing memories. Commander Shigefuso Hashimoto told American interrogators that "In the first five or ten minutes of action, the *Nachi* was hit at the after end of the bridge by a blue dye-loaded shell, which killed five or six communications personnel and wounded twelve or thirteen others." The significance of Hashimoto's statement is that the *Salt Lake City*'s projectiles were loaded with blue dye while the *Richmond*'s were loaded with orange dye. The attribution of the hits to the *Richmond* because only two shells hit is also open to debate: given the normal dispersion of a salvo, and the fact that two of the *Salt Lake City*'s four turrets were two-gun turrets, two hits would seem in no way to exclude the heavy cruiser.[67]

There are three other significant factors in the *Salt Lake City*'s favor: her main battery control personnel had seen more combat than their counterparts in the *Richmond*, her control personnel were afforded a better view of the enemy, and her guns had a longer effective range. Experience tells in war, just as it does in all other endeavors. All of the *Salt Lake City*'s control officers had been in combat, whereas this was the first ship-to-ship action for the *Richmond*. At the time of the hits, the *Salt Lake City*'s guns were being controlled by the forward director, a position affording a much better view of the enemy than the *Richmond*'s after director, which was controlling the latter ship's battery. When the level of experience in the *Salt Lake City*'s control station is taken into account, as well as the amount of time that passed between sighting the Japanese heavy cruisers and the order to open fire, it is clear that a good initial firing solution should have been available.

The factor of effective range is perhaps the most crucial. Ranges of artillery, land-based and naval, are measured in terms of maximum and effective ranges. Maximum range is the greatest distance a projectile can be made to travel. Effective range is the distance that a projectile can be made to travel with any reasonable degree of accuracy. The 6"/53 guns with which the *Richmond* was armed had a maximum range of about 22,000 yards but an effective range of only 14,000 yards. The 8"/55 guns with which the *Salt Lake City* was armed had a maximum range of just over 30,000 yards but an effective range of 19,500 yards. The radar track of the battle shows the 0845 range to the Japanese to be about 16,000 yards from the *Salt Lake City* and about 18,000 yards from the *Richmond*. The professional competence of the *Richmond*'s gunners is not in question. It is simply that they were shooting at extreme range with an antiquated weapons system. The chance of a two-shell salvo scoring under those circumstances is so remote as to be improbable. Ralph Millsap's assertion that the hits halved Japanese firepower is entirely correct, and his pride in his ship is understandable. However, the evidence says that the first hits on the *Nachi* came from the *Salt Lake City*'s guns.[68]

Around 0852, Hosogaya finally turned his heavy cruisers to the southwest in pursuit of the Americans. Light cruiser *Tama* took the inside of the turn, opening out to 4,000 yards on the starboard side of the *Nachi*. The *Abukuma* and her tail of destroyers also cut inside the turn and steadied up slightly northward and astern of the *Tama*. All the light units were now off the *Nachi*'s starboard side. Most Japanese attention, and nearly all Japanese gunfire, was now focused on the *Salt Lake City*, which was slightly off the *Nachi*'s port bow and about ten miles ahead. Hosogaya next ordered his destroyers to open to port with the intention of delivering a torpedo attack. Like McMorris's order to launch aircraft, this one was never carried out. Kintaro Miura says the destroyers could not make over 28 knots, while Shigefuso Hashimoto says they missed a signal ordering speed increased, thereby falling too far behind to execute the order. At no time during the battle did the Japanese destroyermen exhibit any of their usual elan. It was a failing for which McMorris and his captains were grateful and which later led to speculation that perhaps war losses had made the enemy overcautious.

At 0851, the following message was sent to Admiral Kinkaid: CCD1 TO CTF 16 ENEMY COMPOSED TWO HEAVIES TWO LIGHTS FOUR DESTROYERS TWO TRANSPORTS FM COMCRUDIV ONE TO TASK FORCE CMDR.

82

At 0854, the *Nachi* launched her Jake spotting plane to port. McMorris witnessed the launch as did men on the *Salt Lake City* and the *Coghlan*. The turn to the southwest was successful in opening the range, but it brought only a slight respite from enemy fire. The range had opened beyond the reach of the destroyers, but the *Maya*, the *Salt Lake City*, and the light cruisers continued to trade salvos. At 0856, the smaller splashes raised by the *Tama* and the *Abukuma* caused Rodgers to radio to McMorris, "These are five-inch shells. These are five-inch cruisers." It is not recorded if McMorris felt any consolation. At 0858, he ordered speed increased to 30 knots in an attempt to open the range still farther. As her engineers answered the call for increased speed, a momentarily too heavy flow of fuel to the boilers caused black smoke to pour from the *Salt Lake City*'s stacks. Eager for evidence of a hit, the Japanese mistakenly entered this smoke as "Enemy's heavy cruiser on fire."[69]

At 0900, the invisible menace represented by the *Nachi*'s torpedoes showed itself. Lookouts on the American flagship reported torpedoes passing under the bow. Nothing in their experience had prepared either McMorris or Waldschmidt for the possibility of such long-range weapons, so they chose to attribute the reports of torpedoes to a school of fish. Little did they know that the torpedoes were very real. Worthy Bitler saw a wake from his position on the *Salt Lake City*'s open bridge. Ralph Millsap later heard from one of the ship's engineers that a torpedo had been heard passing under the ship. John Atkeson's Action Report mentions a torpedo broaching 4,000 yards on the *Bailey*'s port quarter at about the same time. The most convincing testimony comes from the *Richmond*'s Gene Purdy and Jerry Miller:

> [Purdy] When the encounter started, I was standing on the port side of the pilothouse. The enemy was to starboard. Someone on the starboard side yelled, "Torpedo amidships." I looked straight down into the water and saw the torpedo wake come out from under the ship and head out to sea—away from the enemy. After the battle, the gunnery yeoman asked me if I

Yeoman 2c Gene Purdy, phone talker, *Richmond*.   Courtesy Gene
Purdy

had seen that S.O.B. go under us. It struck terror in [us] and
I am satisfied that if that torpedo had been a few feet shallower,
[the] part about the *Richmond* would end there.[70]
[Miller] It was a clear day. It was a calm sea. I knew something
about torpedoes, not that we ever fired that many, but I knew
something about the torpedo business. I had seen some wakes
and I knew what a torpedo wake was. Standing up in that
foretop, I *know* I saw a torpedo wake go right under the bridge
of the *Richmond* . . . at almost a 90° angle. It was a beautiful
shot. It was just too deep. When the action was over and I

tried to make that point, and several others confirmed that they'd seen torpedo wakes, we were kind of pooh-poohed by the brass. [Nobody thought] we'd got in close enough to launch torpedoes. There isn't any question that I saw a torpedo wake go under the *Richmond*.[71]

Luck was with the Americans. None of these torpedoes, each capable of gutting a ship, struck home. At 0903, the *Richmond* ceased fire. The range had opened to such an extent that any further firing was purely a waste of ammunition. At 0907, the *Maya* fired four torpedoes from her starboard tubes. Fortune continued to smile on the Americans because all missed. The Japanese ships were now on McMorris's port quarter, ten to eleven miles back. Samuel Eliot Morison says that the *Maya* was keeping up a high rate of fire and dropping many near misses around the *Salt Lake City*. George O'Connell agrees that the Japanese cruiser was lashing the sea around his ship, but says she was maintaining a very poor salvo interval.

Jim Brewer remembers watching with a sense of professional detachment. He was dressed in a like outfit to that already described by George O'Connell and also wore a sound-powered phone set. He was on the *Salt Lake City*'s open bridge in company with Captain Rodgers and Worthy Bitler. Jim Brewer had graduated from Annapolis in 1927, but resigned in 1929 to make his way in civilian life. War was looming when he reentered the Navy in 1940. He laughingly refers to himself as a "Goddam Reserve" who had a lot of work to do to catch up with his peers. Evidence that he did catch up is found in the fact that he was made the gunnery officer in the summer of 1942. As he recalls that March morning in 1943, he remembers feeling that the problem posed by the distant Japanese was no more than an artillery duel between professionals. He was shooting at their machines, they were shooting at his, and neither could do anything to stop the heavy shells from coming down. His phones allowed him to stay in close touch with all gunnery stations, and by remaining with the captain he was able to warn George O'Connell of impending

changes of course and speed. Not too surprisingly, he says
that his entire world had narrowed down to the patch of ocean
that held the enemy ships.[72]

Not so professionally detached were the hundreds of men
in all the ships who had stations topside. They were the men
manning the torpedo tubes, the antiaircraft guns, the secondary batteries in the cruisers, the searchlights, and the smoke
generators. All they could do was stare wide-eyed as salvo
after salvo plowed up the ocean around them. Bosun's mate
1c Alex Mihalka, a gun captain on the *Salt Lake City*'s fantail
40-mm guns, says the approaching shells ". . . sounded like
a freight train." Seaman 1c Rod Woolworth, a shellman on
one of the cruiser's 5-inch guns, tells what he saw:

> I personally did not fully realize what was taking place until I
> went over near the ammo hoist amidships. At that time, the
> Japs were on our port quarter about twelve to fifteen miles
> back. I looked in that direction in time to see them fire a salvo
> of orange-grey fire. Shortly thereafter, eight or ten shells ripped
> up the port side. Needless to say, most of us became as scared
> as anyone can get. The sound of those shells hitting close aboard
> is a sound that is difficult to describe. It's unbelievable. Our
> gun captain saw our state of affairs so he had each of us take
> a 5-inch shell and sit on the deck with it in our laps; this to
> occupy our minds and give us something to do. The only thing
> was, he sat us amidships facing aft. We could look up at any
> time and see those eight or ten shells appear and then rip up
> one side or another.[73]

Woolworth was one of many men who had the distinct impression that he could see the enemy shells as they streaked into
the water. Jim Brewer likens what he saw to seeing rainfall
out of the corner of one's eye. Chuck Harrison had the vivid
impression of seeing a shell burst in the water. These fleeting
impressions were unforgettably buttressed by the thunder-
claps that followed the arrival of the enemy salvos. One salvo
roared over the *Salt Lake City*'s bridge so deafeningly that a
sailor near Worthy Bitler reflexively flinched. Bitler remem-

Chief Bosun's Mate Alex Mihalka, gun captain, *Salt Lake City*.   Courtesy Alex Mihalka

bers that Captain Rodgers turned to the man with a big grin and told him, "Don't worry, you won't hear the one that gets you."[74]

The radiomen in both American cruisers were also busy. While Ralph Millsap and his men were dealing with the ad-

Seaman 1c Rod Woolworth, 5-inch shell man,
Salt Lake City.   Courtesy Rod Woolworth

miral's contact and subsequent reports to Adak, the radiomen
in the *Salt Lake City* were trying to summon help from the air
base on Amchitka. Their first call on a voice net was answered
with an immediate "Go ahead." Amchitka was told to wait
while an up-to-the-minute position report was made up. When
the next call was made, there was no answer. After several
unanswered repetitions on the voice circuit, a coded message
giving the ship's position and the type of assistance required
was tapped out in the blind on a CW circuit. There was no

confirmation or reply, but the message *was* received because it later appeared on the fleet broadcast from Naval Radio Station San Francisco. Naval radiomen are constantly being reminded that they are a most vital link with higher authority and with help. Nothing is more baffling or frustrating to them than to establish contact with a station and then inexplicably lose that contact.

Shortly after the turn to the southwest, the *Salt Lake City* suffered the first of a series of mechanical failures that would plague her throughout the battle. The turn had brought the forward turrets up against their training stops, no longer able to bear on the enemy. The turn also brought the forward director, which was built before the days of electrical slip rings, to the limit of its travel. While it was being rotated back to the port side, control of the after two turrets was momentarily passed to Director II. With no warning, the director trainer's telescope suffered a mechanical failure, rendering it useless for the rest of the day. Turrets III and IV immediately shifted to local control in train, but local control inevitably meant a degradation in accuracy. As soon as the ship settled on the new course, control of the turrets was switched back to Director I.

In the ship's newly installed CIC, a team of plotters and evaluators under the direction of Chet Lee was keeping a running plot of the battle. They were also doing their best to help the gunners by phoning radar ranges to the directors. Their plotting efforts, which resulted in the first track chart of a battle based on radar data, were more successful than their efforts to help the gunners. They were thwarted time and again in this latter effort by 1943 state of the art in electronics. The SG surface-search radar mounted on the *Salt Lake City* provided reliable range data, but had no input to the range-keepers. Radar ranges were a useful backup, but visual data remained paramount. The Mark 3 and Mark 4 fire control radars that were mounted on the ship were rendered ineffective by a combination of gunfire shock and electrical failures.[75]

At 0908, the *Nachi*'s spotting plane ventured close enough to the *Richmond*'s port side for her to open fire with her 3-inch battery. Only seven rounds were fired before the plane veered off. Peter Gaviglio noted in his Action Report that it was more a gesture designed to relieve tension among the exposed gun crews than a real attempt to down the plane. The Japanese airmen also evaded a thirty-two-round barrage flung at them by the *Monaghan*. At 0910, McMorris directed the *Dale* and the *Monaghan* to move up from the *Salt Lake City*'s port quarter and join the *Richmond*. This order was fine with Ken Robinson. Only a minute before, he had told his skipper, "Captain, we better get the hell out between *Salt Lake City* and the Japs."[76] The short-falling rounds of enemy salvos were crashing around the *Dale*, inundating her topsides and spattering her with shrapnel. Radioman 3c Charles Abrams says the shock of these near misses was enough to make a man consider ". . . going over the hill at the next opportunity."[77] Ken Robinson's wish to be out of the way was granted as the two destroyers complied with McMorris's order.

In the same moment that McMorris was maneuvering his destroyers, the *Maya* landed a shell so close aboard the *Salt Lake City*'s port side that Rodgers thought his ship had been hit. Morison's account lists this near miss as a hit, but he is again in error. Morison feels that the *Salt Lake City* was hit on her starboard catapult at 0910. Rodgers's Action Report records the hit on the catapult as coming at 1059. McMorris's report and Al Ovrum's chronology cite the heavy cruiser's aircraft on fire and subsequently jettisoned at 1059 and 1100, respectively. It was only a near miss that shook the *Salt Lake City* at 0910.[78]

Damage-control parties were still looking for any signs of a hit when the sharp rap of the cruiser's 5-inch guns began to reverberate through her hull. The enemy spotter plane was making another appearance. The *Dale* and the *Monaghan* also opened up, quickly causing the plane to veer off. In the distance, the *Nachi* suddenly gave off a gout of smoke and began to slow. The *Salt Lake City*'s Action Report claims a hit at 0920 and John Atkeson's report is in agreement. According to *A Battle History of the Imperial Japanese Navy*, the *Nachi*'s Action Report records hits at 0850 and 1148 only. Nonetheless, the enemy flagship was observed to give off a gout of smoke that seemed commensurate with a hit. As she began to slow, the *Maya* checked fire and slowed with her. This latest act of apparent indecision and confusion on the part of the enemy commander caused McMorris to turn his attentions to the Japanese transports. They had long since vanished over the northern horizon, but McMorris now took the opportunity to begin working his task group around to a northerly course. Whether he really believed he could get to the transports is knowledge that died with McMorris. Nevertheless, both he and his captains recorded that the way in which the Japanese force was fought led them to believe that the first hit on the *Nachi*'s bridge had seriously affected the enemy admiral. It was on this basis that McMorris recorded a belief that he might get to the transports.[79]

Around 0925, the *Nachi*'s damage-control personnel finished splicing the electrical leads to the director. Shrapnel from the first hit had severed the cables, but because the ship's generators were still off line, the damage went unnoticed. Even though power was restored to the turrets, the *Nachi*'s guns remained silent until repairs were completed. The *Salt Lake City* was thus granted added minutes of respite, and considering how well the *Nachi* was shooting at the outset, may have changed the course of the battle. The fact that the respite was over was very plainly evident as the enemy flagship added her ten guns to the barrage aimed at the *Salt Lake City*. In this long-range duel of heavy cruisers, the Japanese admiral adopted a tactic that was of the greatest help to the Americans. The *Nachi* and the *Maya* were being steered on zigzag courses, a tactic that allowed them to deliver full salvos, but which negated the 2-knot speed advantage they held over the *Salt Lake City*. Hosogaya's reluctance to use his superior speed to close to a killing range was another inadvertent favor for which the Americans were grateful.

At 0933, the enemy spotting plane braved another approach to the task group. This time, the *Salt Lake City* poured out an eighty-five-round barrage from her starboard 5-inch battery. Gerry Reeves was the officer controlling this barrage. A man with a sense of humor, he writes, "The after AA Control Officer wisely withheld fire until the plane was well within 5-inch gun range and then opened up, damaging the plane and causing it to crash."[80] Though the plane appeared to falter and begin giving off smoke, Reeves's lethal aspirations were thwarted by the time fuzes of 1943. The enemy airmen may have been disconcerted by the 3,000-yard gauntlet of flak thrown up by the *Salt Lake City*, but they later landed at Attu.

Reeves has this to say about the battle itself:

> During the entire engagement, I only worked about five minutes. The rest of the time I watched and listened. My station was the after 5-inch director. My head was out the top of the director where I could see it all. I wore split phones, with one ear tuned to my guns, and the other to the circuit between the Captain and the Gunnery Officer. On the bulkhead behind me was a speaker over which I heard everything that went over the intership voice circuit. I did . . . know at all times what went on, though there were times I would have preferred not to know so much.[81]

Throughout the first hour of the action, the *Abukuma* and her four destroyers had been steaming about 4,000 yards to the north of the enemy heavy cruisers. Around 0935, the Japanese light cruiser suddenly closed to 20,000 yards on the *Salt Lake City*'s starboard quarter. That was close enough for Jim Brewer and George O'Connell; the after turrets were shifted from the *Nachi* to the *Abukuma*. It took but three salvos to deliver the message to Admiral Mori and his men that their presence was unwanted. The *Abukuma* quickly opened the range and the after turrets were again directed on the *Nachi*.

The inability to contribute more was very frustrating to

LT(jg) Gerry Reeves, after AA officer, *Salt Lake City.*   Courtesy
Gerry Reeves

Ben Johnston. He was a 1939 graduate of Annapolis who was
thought of by his fellow officers as formal, rather serious, and
a totally conscientious officer. One of his former shipmates
remembers that the training he received from Ben was instrumental in averting a serious collision at sea. Bob Matusek, who

also served under Johnston, feels Ben was instrumental in turning him into a successful officer. Although line officers of the United States Navy were then expected to be proficient in several fields, Johnston's professional passion was gunnery. To his lasting disgust and frustration, the stern chase meant that Turret I and his Turret II were usually unable to bear. By putting the turret almost against the training stops, there were occasions when he could fire. Each time he *was* able to shoot, he had a momentary pang of pity for the men on the open bridge. The muzzles of Turret II's three guns were almost literally in the faces of the bridge watch when the turret was on its aftermost bearing. The muzzle blast was so intense that one compass repeater was broken from its mounting, and the track chart being kept by Chet Lee and his men, who were *inside* the charthouse, was torn in several places. Johnston tried as hard as he could to keep the turret on a firing bearing, but more often than not, the general direction of the chase kept him blocked out.[82]

Between occasional salvos, the turret crews of Turrets I and II could only stand to their guns and wait. Only the pointer, trainer, and turret officer could see what was happening, and that was through the limited perspective of their sights. All hands could feel the shock of the many near misses falling around the ship. Some of the shocks were so severe that Johnston more than once felt the turret was trying to lift off the roller path. After one particularly severe shock, "I opened my door to look out, sure that I wouldn't see anything left out there." The just receding splashes raised by the enemy salvo were so close that he quickly closed the turret door. The closeness of the enemy shells had left him inwardly shaken, but he told the men in the gun chamber that they ". . . had missed by a mile." As proud of the *Salt Lake City*'s ability to shoot as he was, he was equally impressed by the tightness of the Japanese patterns. "You could have held a barrel hoop out there and they would have all gone through the same hoop."[83]

94

Johnston's words are an obvious exaggeration, of course, but all the American officers were impressed with the technical prowess of the Japanese. Lieutenant Mike Callahan, the *Dale's* director officer, writes, "I was surprised with the alignment of the Japanese batteries—nine shells would drop with no more dispersion than the width of a two-lane concrete road."[84] Howard Grahn estimates that the Japanese salvos fell in a pattern no more than 15 × 45 yards. In comparison, the *Salt Lake City's* patterns were usually in the neighborhood of 50 × 350 yards. The Japanese salvos were so tight that impact circles in the water intersected. Grahn very vividly remembers a voice on the phone circuit, which he is sure was Lyle Ramsey, exclaiming, "Christ, what a pattern! Christ, what a pattern!"[85] Grahn and his shipmates might have found some consolation in the knowledge that they were causing some anxiety aboard the Japanese flagship. Blue-dyed shell splashes kept the *Nachi's* bridge well drenched and later caused Kintaro Miura to blame smarting eyes on the dye.

The mental discomfiture being suffered by Ben Johnston and his turret crew was nothing in comparison to the acute physical discomfort being suffered by the men manning the fantail 40-mm guns. The five 8-inch guns of the after turrets were firing directly over their heads. The tremendous overpressure of the muzzle blasts was literally battering them to the deck. Gun shields were bent, sights wrecked, and ammo made unserviceable. These men had grown inured to hardship; the after gun tubs were so often awash that they jokingly said they deserved submarine pay. This battering was too much, however, and they were finally told to take shelter below deck. The same sort of problem was being experienced in the *Dale.* Her after two 5-inch guns had no gun shield of any sort; when range caused the opening fusillade to be broken off, Gun III was firing directly over the heads of the men on Gun IV. Ken Robinson remembers the gunnery officer frequently asking for enough of a course change to allow the guns to train out some and relieve the torment of Gun IV's crew. There was no question of abandoning the gun, but the gun crew was fortunate in the sense that the range was usually too long for them to shoot.[86]

By every account, Bertram Rodgers was doing a superb job of conning his ship. Every naval officer was taught the tactic of chasing salvos; Rodgers was turning it into something of an art form on that morning. Successful salvo chasing requires good timing and a healthy degree of intuition on the part of the conning officer. The tall man atop the *Salt Lake City*'s pilothouse was displaying both to the point of uncanniness. Time after time, he would alter course and a salvo would smash into the spot just vacated. He said that when he assumed command of the ship, "I felt like I was a plebe at the Naval Academy. I took over and before I got a breath taken, I was up in this fighting—it was a hell of a transition for me." No man who witnessed his coolness under fire will ever agree with his characterization of himself as a plebe. His baptism of fire was marked by an aura of cool professionalism that was an inspiration to all around him. It has been reported that after one particularly close miss, Rodgers turned to his exec and asked, "Well, Worthy, which way do I go this time?" Both Rodgers and Worthy Bitler said this is an accurate representation.[87] A thread common to the recollections of many of the *Salt Lake City*'s men is found in their captain's assertion that he did what he had to do and trusted in the Lord's help. Like an elusive running back, his ship was weaving and turning through clusters of maroon and blue-tinged shell splashes, trying to avoid a lethal tackle. Her radical maneuvering was causing her to lag farther behind the *Richmond*, now some 3,000 to 4,000 yards ahead.

The pressing need to keep the enemy under as heavy a fire as possible led McMorris to make a wise decision. At 0945, he gave Rodgers permission to maneuver his ship in whatever way necessary to best utilize her firepower. Task group course and speed remained the admiral's prerogative, but the *Richmond* thereafter conformed to the movements of the *Salt Lake City*.

96

With McMorris's recent order in mind, Rodgers, his gun boss, and George O'Connell were keeping a wary eye on the *Abukuma*. The Japanese light cruiser was again slowly creeping up on the starboard quarter in an apparent attempt to gain a spotting position for the *Nachi* and the *Maya*. When the range to the enemy ship had narrowed to 18,000 yards, Rodgers ordered the helm thrown hard over to the right, unmasking the forward turrets.

With a "We'll get this son of a bitch," from Jim Brewer, all ten guns spat out a full salvo. As electric motors purred, pulling the guns down to their loading elevation of 5°, a blast of high-pressure air was jetted into the bore of each gun,

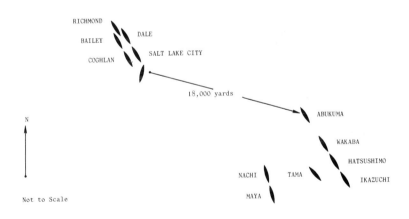

Figure 3. 0953—26 March 1943; *Salt Lake City* fires 8 salvos at *Abukuma*.

purging any potentially lethal embers left after the previous shot. Ten loading trays slammed down into position. Ten 256-pound, armor-piercing shells were tipped from the hoists and power rammed into the gun breeches. Powder-box doors snapped open and the silken bags were quickly passed to the guns. Up went the loading trays. As the last breech in each turret twisted shut, the turret officer threw his Turret Ready switch over the *ready* position. Only twelve seconds had passed. As the second *ready* light flashed on in the director, the director pointer pulled the trigger. Eight salvos blasted out in quick succession, flinging some ten tons of steel and high explosives at the *Abukuma*. Spurred by adrenalin, the turret crews worked with such speed that no turret got out of synch with the others. This barrage had the desired intimidating effect. To the astonishment of the watching Americans, the enemy light cruiser heeled into a 360° turn before again steadying up in pursuit. No hits were scored, but the *Abukuma* was given a good shaking. After the eighth salvo, the *Salt Lake City* turned back to the west, again blocking the forward turrets out.

This rapid-fire cannonade drew more than one man's attention to the guns, though each had different interests. Howard Grahn could see sea spray turning to steam as it hit the barrels of the after turrets. In Jerry Engle's Turret IV, the turret captain made the whimsical observation that he wondered what the bridge would say to the old dictum that firing should be suspended after so many rounds to let the barrels cool off. At the same time, George O'Connell remembers ordering all turrets to begin shooting only one gun per salvo. He had grown increasingly concerned about the high rate at which the ship's 1,250-round supply of armor-piercing shot was being depleted. Only two guns firing meant a negligible chance of a hit, but O'Connell wanted to have some ammo left when the decisive moment arrived.[88]

More than an hour had passed since the first Japanese salvo geysered the sea around the *Richmond*. A contact report

98

and an amplifying report had been radioed to headquarters, but no one there knew for certain if a battle had developed. The hands of the clock were climbing toward 1000 when another message from McMorris began to come in:

MY ZERO NINE THIRTY POSIT LAT FIFTY THREE DASH EIGHTEEN LONG ONE SIX EIGHT DASH TEN MY COURSE 300 X ENGAGED AT EXTREME RANGE

Spare in its wording, the message brought the vital news that battle had been joined. As the message passed from hand to hand on its way to Admiral Kinkaid, no one who handled it could know the peril expressed in the words, "Engaged at extreme range."

At 0958, McMorris ordered course 025° and slowed the formation to 28 knots. The enemy spotting plane popped out of the clouds on the *Richmond*'s starboard side, only to draw another seventeen rounds of antiaircraft fire. It turned back into the murk as quickly as it had emerged. All hands knew by this time that the American force was running for its life. Even so, an aura of calm pervaded all six ships. Worthy Bitler's normal battle station was in the after conning station, but he had received permission from Captain Rodgers to roam at will throughout the ship. Everywhere he went he saw concern, but surprisingly, no outward displays of fear. The senior man in the after conning station while Bitler was absent was Chuck Vasey. During one of the exec's visits to the bridge, Vasey became very concerned that should a shell hit the bridge, he would be temporarily in control of the ship. The thought bothered him as much as the hail of enemy shells falling around the *Salt Lake City*. Father Hodge was also in constant motion throughout the ship. The Padre, as he was always called, clasped his rosary beads in a mittened hand and calmly walked from station to station, offering words of solace and encouragement to all. Between turns around the ship, he sat in Bitler's stateroom to meditate and pray. The memory of his always calm presence is sharp in the recollections of the men. He says he wasn't worried for the simple reason that he didn't realize the enormity of the situation.[89]

Bob Walker of the *Bailey* writes, "I think the term *worried* might be appropriate here. Scared seems too strong, but when you are facing death, who really has the proper word? Basically, you are too busy making sure you do your job to support the ship that you don't have the time to be scared."[90] Frank Ayers had a feeling of detachment: "I was too young, excited, and ignorant to be frightened. I was in the position of an interested bystander seeing everything that was going on but detached from it. The thought that we might be sunk at any moment didn't occur to me."[91] It was a scene played out dozens of times over in all six ships. As exposed as they were, the men topside were allowed the natural relief of being able to see what was happening. The hundreds of men with stations below decks had to rely on phoned reports or an occasional account from someone who had been topside. For those men not busy tending machinery or handling ammunition, the minutes passed very slowly.

Others with stations below were more fortunate. The engineers were fully occupied. The knowledge that the ship was dependent on them for the power to move and shoot kept them closely wedded to their machinery and too busy to be much concerned with outside events. George Ales writes about the scene in the *Richmond*'s after engine room:

> As best as I can remember, the after engine room personnel were calm, maybe somewhat apprehensive, excited and I'm sure all of us had butterflies in our stomachs. I did. Everyone went about his duties as required, very efficiently [with] no goofing off or horse play. There wasn't any appearance of being scared or terrified.[92]

One man, Water Tender 2c Elmer "Rebel" Duren of the *Dale*, didn't *want* to see what was happening: "One time, the chief offered to relieve me while I went topside to watch a while, but I said 'No thanks'—I had no desire to see the enemy ships shooting at us."[93]

Some men, of course, do not stand the strain of combat as well as others. Seaman 1c Al Melville, in Number II handling room on the *Salt Lake City*, remembers one such man:

> During the action, our new man on the phone could not talk and looked scared stiff. He was pale and sweaty. We thought it was his new battle station so we didn't make anything of it. We were singing and figuring we were really kicking the hell out of the Japs. Powder was moving up, our turret was rotating, and it felt like we were doing a lot of firing.

Seaman 1c Jack Bacues,one of the 40-mm gunners who had been driven below, saw one man leaning against a bunk with a blanket pulled over his head, ". . . as if this would stop a shell." The drawn looks on the faces of many of his comrades caused one sailor in the *Salt Lake City*'s after repair party to chidingly say, "What's the matter with you guys, you look like it's your last day on earth."[94]

Firecontrolman 1c Dick Graffius of the *Monaghan* had a decidedly unpleasant experience: "We had a fire controlman . . . who refused to stay on his battle station on the main battery director during this battle. His station was on the stable element, and his job was to take over this unit in manual control if it failed in automatic. Thank Christ it didn't." Though his words were written for himself, the feelings expressed by Gerry Reeves doubtlessly speak for many men of the task group:

> I had always wondered how I would behave if, under heavy fire, I suddenly realized that death was certain or imminent. Would I wave a sword and say something which would go down in history for generations of midshipmen to hear about? Would I cry and scream and hide under something? What happened surprised me . . . I got very calm, very quiet, and

very sad; all I could think of was the things I had never gotten
to do and never would get to do—marry a nice girl—hold a
son. . . .[95]

By 1000, the American task group had been under continuous
fire for nearly an hour and a half. Several hundred Japanese
shells had fallen around the American ships, with most directed at the *Salt Lake City*. All six ships had been shaken by
near misses, but none had been hit. What no man could know
was that the worst part of the day's ordeal was about to begin.
Just after four bells struck, the outlook began to darken om-
inously.

With some concern, Admiral McMorris observed the *Salt
Lake City* begin to steer erratically. Captain Rodgers shortly
radioed the task force commander with the unsettling news
that his ship had lost rudder control. Gunfire shock had caused
the hydraulic limit stops to fail with the rudder hard over to
the right. The heavy cruiser continued veering to the right,
out of control. It is not too hard to imagine the alarm of the
helmsman as he spun the big wheel and got no response. In
Director II, Howard Grahn's most experienced phone talker
quietly nudged him. Not wishing to alarm the new men in
the director, he whispered to Grahn that the ship had lost
rudder control. Grahn was a reader of naval history and had
a quick flash of the battering suffered by the HMS *Warspite*
when she had a similar casualty at Jutland. It was not a com-
forting thought.[96] Steering control was shifted to after steering, but for a long moment, before steering room personnel
could regain control, the rudder continued to oscillate. Because
of fears that the hydraulic system would fail again, the rudder
was arbitrarily limited to angles of 10° or less. It was a potentially dangerous limitation, given the need of the ship to
maneuver freely.

Japanese main battery control officers may have divined
some trouble in the *Salt Lake City*'s wayward meanderings
because their fire increased in volume and the American ship

was again straddled repeatedly. A few salvos were also tossed at the *Richmond*, but did her no harm. The increased rate of fire may have been in response to an order from Hosogaya directing his entire force to press home the attack. Both Japanese heavy cruisers were observed to increase speed, and the range was soon under 20,000 yards. The problem, if any, that caused the *Nachi* to slow had obviously been cleared up. While the steering room personnel were struggling with the rudder, George O'Connell opportunistically took advantage of the surprise turn to order ten gun salvos. When the return to course again forced the forward turrets to lay out, O'Connell directed the after turrets to continue shooting all guns. He was going to do his best to dissuade the Japanese from getting *too* close.

Adversity is a constant shipmate in wartime. O'Connell no sooner issued his orders to the after turrets than George Halvorsen reported from Director I that the rangekeeper was not accepting spots and that the elevation gears were slipping. Without missing a beat, O'Connell called, "All stations, Control. Shift director control to Director II, continue director fire collective. Spot One spot." Salvos continued to crash out at their steady pace. For the time being, the battery remained under the control of Howard Grahn in Director II. Hardworking technicians were able to correct the electrical malfunctions, but turret pointers thereafter had to assume local control when Director I was controlling the battery.[97]

The sum of the failures in the directors was that the turret officers were burdened with setting up a good part of the fire control solution. Depending on which director was controlling the battery, the turret officer was responsible for the guns of his turret being properly laid for deflection or range. He had to very quickly assimilate the estimated target data being furnished by the radarmen, the spotting officer, his own observations made through the turret periscope, and the data being generated by the turret rangekeeper. At some point, information, seaman's eye, and experience came together in orders affecting point, train, and the turning on of the *Ready* light.

Jerry Engle's Turret IV spent most of the battle in local control, so he is well qualified to tell what it was like:

> As far as local control is concerned, we lost fire direction from the after director almost at the outset of the battle and were in local control for the rest of the fight. While we were in Pearl Harbor for refit, Lyle Ramsey had secured some old Ford instruments and we had one in each turret booth. My junior turret officer was manning this machine and feeding me information to correct the sights after our projectiles landed and I did the spotting for them. Without these Baby Fords, our fire could not have been as good as it was. At that time, we were in communication with Control on sound-powered phones, which performed well. However, inside the turret, we were still using the old voice tubes to the turret captain, the pointer and trainer. As time went by, it became almost impossible to be heard over the noise of the guns and with our diminishing voice power, making it very difficult to coach the pointer and trainer onto target when it was obscured from them.[98]

Despite these difficulties, it is a measure of her gunners' skill that the *Salt Lake City's* blue-dyed splashes remained tantalizing close to the *Nachi* and the *Maya* throughout the morning.

Shortly after 1000, an unwittingly humorous message was received from headquarters:

MAKING READING WITH AIR X SUGGEST FOR YOUR CONSIDERATION RETIRING ACTION TO PROVIDE OPPORTUNITY TO OFFSET WITH AIR YOUR INFERIOR STRENGTH X KINKAID TO MCMORRIS X PRESENT BEST ESTIMATE ARRIVAL FIRST BOMBING GROUP 1430 X CATALINAS SHOULD ARRIVE EARLIER

McMorris recorded that this message brought a laugh to the men on the *Richmond's* bridge, but he knew there was little humor in the situation he was facing. Bombers arriving five hours hence might well find nothing but wreckage on the sea. After 1003, when the *Salt Lake City's* ability to maneuver became so limited, the tenor of the chase changed drastically.

The slim hope that the Japanese transports could be caught had to go by the board. She was by no means crippled, but the *Salt Lake City*'s steering handicap was grave enough to make escape the paramount concern.

THE BATTLE: 1005–1155

Faced with the *Salt Lake City*'s steering problem, Mc-Morris decided that the only judicious course of action was to disengage his task group as soon as possible. However, as he later wrote, ". . . the disengagement did not prove too easy of accomplishment."[99] At 1005, he ordered course 350°. He wanted to turn to the south, but the enemy was too obviously in a position to cut him off. The Americans had to continue to the westward, hoping a favorable opportunity to break away would arise. At 1007, the *Abukuma*'s torpedomen made an attempt to slow the headlong flight of the American line. Four more of the huge Long Lance torpedoes were sent churning on their way, but once again, none struck home.

At 1010, Japanese gunners finally scored a direct hit on the *Salt Lake City*. An 8-inch shell slammed into the foc's'le, pierced the main deck, crashed through the chain locker, and still without exploding, deflected out the starboard side below the waterline. Except to a few men in the forwardmost stations, this hit was felt only as a slight tremor that passed through the ship. Even the men closest to the hit weren't sure. Seaman 1c Jerry Rodebaugh, who was on the shell deck of Turret I, recalls that there was a difference of opinion among the men working there: "When we took our first hit, the whole ship shuddered. Bosun's Mate Beeson said it was a big wave. I said, 'Bullshit, we got hit.' That was our first taste of action."[100] Damage control personnel were quickly at the scene and as a precautionary measure, shored bulkhead Number 10. Flooding was limited to five small compartments, and although the ship was thereafter a little down by the head, her speed was unimpaired.

Unlike the infantryman's war, in which natural features

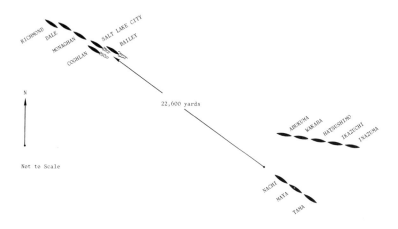

Figure 4. 1018—26 March 1943; TG 16.6 begins to make smoke.

of the terrain offer cover, there is no concealment other than foul weather on a seascape. With the advent of the oil-fueled warship came an easily controlled means of creating artificial concealment. By reducing the air supply and increasing the oil flow to a boiler, dense clouds of black smoke could be created. Weather conditions, especially the wind, had to be favorable for a smoke screen to be efficacious. On that Friday morning in the North Pacific, weather conditions were ideal. Immediately after the hit on his ship, Captain Rodgers suggested to the task force commander that the destroyers begin laying a smoke screen. At 1013, McMorris slowed the task group to 25 knots, ordered course 300°, and directed the *Bailey* and the *Coghlan* to assume station on the *Salt Lake City*. Both destroyers showed an increased froth of white under their counters as they peeled away from the flagship. The *Bailey* took a position on the heavy cruiser's starboard quarter and the *Coghlan* on her port beam. The stacks of all three ships began belching clouds of thick, black smoke at 1018. Chemical smoke generators on the fantail of each ship were also activated, adding their acrid white smoke to the screen. The smoke cascading over the after section of each ship made the atmosphere decidedly less pleasant to breathe, but is doubtful if any of the men over whom the smoke was rolling complained. The smoke had barely begun to uncoil behind the American ships when Japanese eyes thought they saw the flash of a hit on the *Salt Lake City*. There was none, but the *Nachi*'s Action Report claims a hit at 1020. At 1028, the task group turned to course 240° to take better advantage of the smoky curtain.

Though the smoke was lying well, the hoped for hindering of Japanese fire control wasn't evident. Whenever the Japanese control officers got even a glimpse of the *Salt Lake City*, their fire was rapid and their shells close aboard. It was so accurate that McMorris and Ralph Riggs felt at least one of the Japanese cruisers had to have radar. As already noted, none of the Japanese ships was so equipped. After countless drills and sixteen months of war, the Japanese gunners were simply very good at their jobs. Fortunately for the *Salt Lake City*, so were her engineers. The diesel-powered emergency steering unit built with such foresight while in Pearl Harbor had to be activated when the rudder driving engine suddenly unclutched. The switchover was made so quickly that no loss of rudder control was experienced.

Around 1030, Hosogaya ordered the *Abukuma* to cross astern of the *Nachi* and come up to the south of the flagship. The destroyers *Ikazuchi* and *Inazuma* signaled that they could no longer keep up with the *Abukuma* and reduced speed to 28 knots. At 1035, McMorris ordered the two destroyers still with the *Richmond* to form on the *Salt Lake City* and begin making smoke. While they were circling around to come up behind the *Coghlan*, John Atkeson brought the *Bailey* sharply across the *Salt Lake City*'s bow to take up the lead position in line. McMorris also ordered Ralph Riggs to assume tactical command of the destroyers. The blanket of smoke generated by five ships had the desired effect: enemy fire slackened perceptibly. George O'Connell's station in Control Forward was nearly 140 feet above the waterline, giving him the best seat in the house. He describes the lull:

> Conn gave me the conn of the ship to coach the destroyers relative to gaps in the screen and to insure that the *Salt Lake City* was always positioned to maximum advantage with respect to the screen. That was wise because I could see the enemy practically all the time. Moreover, with four destroyers smoking, little coaching need be done. We settled down to a slow duel with the heavy cruisers who checked fire, as we did also, each time the *Salt Lake City* became obscured by smoke. Occasionally, a light cruiser tried to sneak around the edge of the screen for an observation, but invariably kept its distance. As the light cruiser peeked around the edge of the screen, we would . . . shoot a few salvos. Usually, that was enough to cause the light cruiser to drift back behind the screen.[101]

At 1044, the *Tama* appeared at the edge of the smoke screen and opened fire on the *Bailey*. These few shots were answered by a furious barrage from the *Bailey*, the *Coghlan*, and the *Richmond*. It was welcome activity for Jerry Miller:

> I . . . remember being frustrated that we could never get into position, a decent range, for firing the guns. I . . . know I was frustrated at having finally gotten into some action after fifteen months of a big war . . . and here was some action, a chance to do some good . . . and I wasn't going to get a chance to get a shot at anybody. It was frustrating.[102]

Miller got to relieve some of that frustration as the *Richmond* pumped out shell after shell at the *Tama*. The enemy light cruiser very quickly turned to the north and disappeared behind the smoke. Even though the range was fairly long, the *Richmond*'s guns continued to fire for the next few minutes at whatever enemy ship poked its bow through the smoke. When she finally ceased fire, a relative lull descended on the combatants. George O'Connell's account continues:

> During this period of the battle . . . the tempo slackened considerably in both the *Salt Lake City* and the enemy heavy cruisers. I even had time to ask a very simple question of one of the telephone talkers on the catwalk with me. He was very young, seventeen years old, from Minnesota. I thought my question was casual, and I expected him to answer with a "Yes" or "No," maybe even a simple grunt. I was not prepared for a sermon, but I got one. "No sir," he replied, "I'm not scared. To be scared you have to have a chance. You are scared because you're going to miss that chance. I don't think we've got a chance. So what could I be scared of? I am sorry for my mother. She doesn't understand, and she's going to take it pretty hard." I got my answer in a lot less time than the telling. We played cat and mouse for what seemed an eternity. We peeked through the gaps on the screen here and there. Director I was . . . the controlling director. Control of the battery was returned to Director I at 1046, and could see the target as well as I.[103]

The lull was put to other uses as well. Chuck Harrison remembers that nearly everyone in the *Richmond*'s after control took the opportunity to relieve the overwhelming desire to urinate. A can was dredged up and passed around. Several emptying trips to the rail had to be made before everyone was accommodated. Ralph Millsap considered getting the ship's camera, but decided he didn't want to compromise her watertight integrity by opening any of the many doors necessary to get to the camera. At 1051, another message was sent to Kinkaid:

CTG 16.6 TO CTF 16 X MCMORRIS SENDS MY COURSE 300 X POSIT 53-42 X 167-40 X STEERING DIFFICULTIES WITH SALT LAKE CITY X TO TASK FORCE CMDR

So far, the task force had been fortunate. Even though the *Salt Lake City* had at times literally disappeared behind the splashes raised by Japanese salvos, no serious damage had been suffered. However, McMorris was very much aware that his course was taking him ever closer to Paramushiro and the threat of Japanese bombers. He knew that somehow, and very soon, the task force had to break away from the seemingly relentless enemy. Like sand in an hour glass, McMorris knew his luck was draining away. In only a few minutes, the sand, and his luck, appeared to be gone.

In the *Monaghan*, a crashing noise so loud that everyone in the space was sure they had been hit, reverberated through the forward engine room. A tooth had broken off the reduction gear, and its passage through the gear housing was creating a fearful cacophony of grinding, crashing noises. The engineering officer was afraid that the whole assembly would disintegrate and ordered the engine slowed. His order was countermanded by Peter Horn, who had phone talker Earl Bangert call down and order the engine back to maximum speed. The reduction gear assembly didn't disintegrate, the noise subsided after a few minutes, and the skipper later assumed full responsibility for the damage to the reduction gear. Equally alarming was a report from the after fire room. The initial contact had caught the *Monaghan* with two cold boilers. Forcing a cold boiler is a tough job, and her engineers had been unlucky; the brickwork in Number IV boiler was severely damaged. With lessened insulation, the boiler casing had heated to incandescence. Like the broken reduction gear, there was no help for it. The *Monaghan* remained in her station, making smoke for the *Salt Lake City*. All four destroyers were in echelon, 800 yards apart and 2,500 yards to port of the heavy cruiser.[104]

At 1059, a little of the phenomenal luck that had so far shielded the *Salt Lake City* from harm deserted her. George O'Connell describes what happened:

> With each sequence of firing, splashes were all around us. Plunging shot whistled past the foretop and splashed just ahead of us. The *Nachi* had found our range and had worked out a good solution. With its tight pattern, it was bound to hit. And hit it did, first at the forward catapult. . . .[105]

Storekeeper 2c Jim Lanman, phone talker, *Salt Lake City*.
Courtesy Jim Lanman

A shell crashed into the engine of the SOC spotter plane sitting on the starboard catapult. The blast of what was judged to be an instantaneously fuzed shell shattered the plane and set the wreckage ablaze. It also sent a hail of shrapnel splashing through the waist of the ship. One fragment ripped into the searchlight platform, mortally wounding Fireman 2c James David. Another fragment traveled athwartships where it hit the base of the port catapult, ricochetted forward to hit a stanchion, ricochetted a few feet back to starboard, and struck the ship's first lieutenant, Lieutenant Commander Windsor Gale. Storekeeper 2c Jim Lanman was standing next to Gale:

> The First Lieutenant and I were standing at the corner of the wardroom, by the rail, when the call came to return to our stations. I turned and took about two steps when I heard a splat, a gasp, and a thud. I turned to see Gale on the deck. I called, "Bearers," stepped to the wardroom door and yelled.[106]

111

Unfortunately, bearers could not help Gale. The fragment that pierced his helmet killed him instantly. His comment during the Dutch Harbor poker game had all too prophetically come true. Several other sailors were also wounded by flying shrapnel. These casualties were soon flooding into the ward-room, which doubled as the Forward Dressing Station. Lan-man was no longer just an interested bystander: "I was the phone talker and the whole scene was very orderly. My cord was long enough that I could assist and everyone who could did just that. One of the stretcher bearers . . . was hit in the throat but didn't know it until one of the corpsmen told him."[107] Two of the wounded were hurt seriously enough to require hospitalization, but Gale and David were the only fatalities suffered by the *Salt Lake City*.

Worthy Bitler headed aft immediately after the hit to assess the damage. He felt his previous experience as damage control officer of the *Pensacola* might be valuable to the men on the scene. Gale had trained his men well, however, and what met the exec's eyes as he reached the scene was a tableau of well-ordered activity. Fire hoses had already been broken out, and cold streams of water were rapidly dousing the fire. As soon as the fire was extinguished, Electrician's Mate 1c Carl Matison and his men on the searchlight platform were called down to help in jettisoning the wreckage. The J-hooks holding the plane to the catapult car were released, all available hands were laid on, and as it started over, the long poles usually used to fend the waterborne plane away from the ship's side were used to propel the wreckage clear. Seeing everything under control, Bitler headed back to the bridge to make his report. No one thought to tell him of the first lieutenant's death.

Other damage caused by the hit was less serious. Myriad holes were punched in the stacks, and one 5-inch gun barrel was badly scored. One fragment ripped unerringly through the after bulkhead of the charthouse to tear through Rodgers's bridgecoat. Another pierced the main deck and wounded a friend of Machinist's Mate 1c Dick McCarthy:

> I recall one of my shipmates answering a call of nature in the heat of the battle and while sitting on the pot, an enemy shell exploded on the well deck above. A piece of shrapnel penetrated the stall he was in, hitting him in the groin. [It] caused a superficial wound for which he eventually received a Purple Heart [and] a lot of kidding. . . .[108]

The hit sent a shudder through the ship, but she did not slow.

The sight of the *Salt Lake City*'s burning plane convinced McMorris that a turn to the south had to be accomplished at once. At 1102, he ordered course 210° and increased speed to 30 knots. The American ships were still leaning into the turn at 1103 when another shell hit the *Salt Lake City*. With what one man described as a ". . . grinding crunch," the 8-inch shell struck at Frame 102 below the waterline on the port side. It deflected off Number 4 propellor shaft, passed through one fuel tank, and exploded in another. Unlike the other two hits, there was no doubt in anyone's mind about what happened. Alex Mihalka says, "When the ship was hit, it shook from stem to stern and felt like it was literally picked out of the water." Jack Bacues likens the hit and after shock to a dog shaking water off its back. Seaman 2c Mike Van Kessel was one of the many newcomers to the ship, but he knew right away what had happened. He was in the crew's mess hall, two decks above the hit:

> We were sitting on the laundry hatch cover and a shell exploded right below us. The compartment flooded with water which I could hear coming in. I said to the Chief, "Water is coming in." With that, he took off forward before I could get the words out of my mouth. This scared me and I went the other way. I soon realized there was no problem in the mess hall so I sat back down. Several shells hit the side [sic] very close to us under water. It sounds like thousands of pinging sounds hitting metal.[109]

No one was injured by this hit, and although the ship seemed to momentarily pause, she did not yet slow. Captain Riggs heard this hit being reported on the TBS and began jockeying his destroyers to within 500 yards of each other in an effort to thicken the smoke screen around the *Salt Lake City*.

The officer in charge of the *Salt Lake City*'s after engine room was Ensign Vince "Shorty" Dahlen. He was a determined former enlisted machinist's mate who had advanced to the commissioned ranks. Like many of the ship's officers, he had been on board since prewar days. With his senses tuned to the various sounds of his machinery, he knew that the ship had already been hit twice. He likened the dimly felt shock to the feeling of hitting some small object in the water, a common occurrence of no consequence. The hit at 1103 was an entirely different story.

The engine room gratings seemed to leap into the air, carrying Dahlen along with them. Rags, tools, coffee mugs, life jackets, and men clattered to the gratings and splashed into the bilges as the destructive energy of the hit whipsawed through the engine room. Blast damage was considerable; it wrapped plating around Number 3 shaft and sprayed shrapnel into several compartments. Flooding quickly engulfed the port shaft alleys, the after gyro room, the antiaircraft switchboard room, the ship's laundry, and the after 5-inch magazine. Most worrisome was the damage suffered to the after fuel service piping, the after bulkhead of the engine room, and the shafts. Both port shafts began to oscillate badly: Number 4 because the shell knocked it out of alignment, and Number 3 because the forward spring bearing was blasted from its mount. As the shafts oscillated, they battered the bulkhead packing glands out of shape, allowing water from the flooded shaft alleys to enter the engine room. Water was also gushing in through a large shrapnel hole in the after bulkhead and around a mass of sprung and distorted piping.[110]

Shorty Dahlen's many years of experience had taught him every nuance and quirk of the ship's machinery. It was knowledge that was now being put to an extreme test. He could see that coping with the damage was clearly beyond the resources of the men in the engine room, so a call for help went out immediately. This call was very quickly answered by Ensign Jim Mew and six men of his damage-control party. Together with Dahlen's men, their first efforts were directed at plugging the hole in the after bulkhead. Low on the bulkhead, the hole was now under water. Pinpointing the main flow was no problem, but the freezing water quickly caused feeling to disappear from hands. The hole was plugged, however, and attention was then turned to the influx around the fuel piping. In a desperate search for some flexible material that could be packed around the individual pipes, some kapok life jackets were cut up and the pieces pounded in around the pipes. This was partially successful, but water continued to seep in. The water gushing through the battered shaft packing glands then became the biggest problem. Nothing could be done to stop the flow as long as the shafts were turning. The hope that the fire and bilge pumps could cope with the flood was dispelled as the water level continued to creep upward. An estimated 700 to 1,000 tons of water caused the ship to take a 5° list to port.[111]

McMorris's next goal was to get his force headed to the east. To that end, he ordered course 180° at 1108. The destroyers had realigned in the turn to the south and all four were now astern of the *Salt Lake City*. At 1110, the *Dale* was treated to some unwanted attention as the *Abukuma* came around the edge of the smoke screen and opened fire. The destroyermen replied in kind and for the next ten minutes, both ships blazed away at each other. Some shells landed within 100 yards of the *Dale*, but she was not hit. The smoke screen intervened around 1120 and the *Dale*'s gunners thankfully ceased fire.

In the *Salt Lake City*'s after engine room, the question of how to cope with the flooding was answered in dramatic though roundabout fashion. No suction was being taken on the two fuel tanks ripped apart by the shell, but fuel was being drawn from tanks farther aft. The piping runs from those tanks were riddled and mangled by blast, allowing seawater to enter the fuel flow. When Shorty Dahlen heard the after fire room was experiencing sputtering boiler fires, he ordered the fuel service shifted to the starboard tanks. The shift was reported to Damage Control Central, but for reasons unknown to Dahlen, an order came back to return to the port service. At 1125, seawater extinguished the boilers in the after fire room. Speed began to drop off rapidly and by 1130, the ship was down to 20 knots.

Dahlen was a man in an unenviable position. Mixed with the 31° seawater was fuel oil from the ruptured tanks. The freezing cold water had thickened the already heavy oil to the consistency of tar, something the fire and bilge pumps were not designed to cope with. Jim Mew's men had added a new submersible pump, but it seemingly made no difference. The water level continued to creep inexorably upward. Dahlen realized that to lose the pumps for even a few minutes would mean disaster. Without hesitation, he ordered the fuel service switched back to starboard. In the after fire room, the contaminated fuel lines were shunted to a waste oil tank, the fuel manifold valved over to the starboard tanks, and a fuel service pump put onto suction. In just a minute, the flow at the test cock showed good oil. One by one, burners in the after four boilers flared into life. As soon as pressure was up sufficiently to roll the starboard engine over, the steam lines were cut in. Number 3 shaft was locked and the main circulator pump applied to the task of lowering the water level. It was none too soon. The water had risen to a level some five feet over the bilge, almost to the turbine casings. The tremendous capacity of the main circulator pump brought quick relief. As the water level receded, the *Salt Lake City*'s speed climbed. She was back to 26 knots, albeit on three engines, by 1135.[112]

Between 1105 and 1115, while Shorty Dahlen and Jim Mew were coping with the *Salt Lake City*'s wounds, the Japanese cruisermen fired sixteen more torpedoes at the American task group. None hit and none were sighted by American

116

lookouts. After the last one was launched, the Japanese ships finally turned to the south. They very quickly began to gain on the slowed *Salt Lake City*. Target angle was such that George O'Connell was able to bring all four turrets to bear. The first full salvo was no sooner on its way than the gremlins that had been plaguing the ship all morning struck again:

> The first salvo was wild—short! The second was wild—short! Director I reported trouble in the rangekeeper. It was not accepting spots. Director control was shifted to Director II. Director II got off two salvos. Director I thought perhaps its trouble had been cleared. I therefore ordered director control shifted back to Director I. Again, the splash was wild. I ordered director control shifted back to Director II. Effective fire was soon regained, although Spot I was required to take into account the swings in deflection. This particular experience with Directors I and II was traced to the hit at Frame 102, which resulted in the flooding of the AA Fire Control Switchboard. Firecontrolman 2c Hill isolated the trouble of "own ship's course" input being received from the switchboard and rerouted the supply from the forward gyroscope. By a process of elimination, Hill managed to eliminate other circuits shorted by the flooded switchboard. Thus, both directors were restored, but I did not risk shifting director control back to Director I. . . .[113]

With radar telling him the range to the enemy was down to 19,000 yards and closing, McMorris ordered Captain Riggs to make a torpedo attack on the advancing enemy. Captain Rodgers broke in on the TBS and requested two destroyers be left with his ship. Riggs ordered the *Dale* to stay with the *Salt Lake City* and directed the others to follow the *Bailey*. The TBS receiver on the *Dale*'s bridge chose that moment to fail; Commander Rorschach didn't hear the order to stay behind and brought his ship around to follow the squadron flagship. Riggs realized what was happening and directed the *Monaghan* to remain behind.

In the *Dale*, Rebel Duren's chief told him, "Hold on to your hat, Rebel, we're going to make a torpedo attack." It was

". . . something I think most destroyermen dreaded, especially against major warships. They concentrate on you with large guns long before you can get close enough to launch your torpedoes. You could tell by the roll of the ship that we were making a sharp turn."[114] The thought of a torpedo attack didn't appeal to Ken Robinson either. As he puts it, "It's damn hard to hit a ship who knows what you're doing."[115] Duren was right about large guns being concentrated on the destroyers. As the Americans wheeled toward him, it was evident to Hosogaya what was intended. Fifth Fleet executed an abrupt turn to starboard, unmasking full batteries to fire on the destroyers. The first shell splashes had begun to sprout up around the *Bailey* and her sisters when Rodgers called McMorris with the happy news that the *Salt Lake City* was working back up to speed. McMorris immediately recalled the destroyers and ordered them to continue screening the force with smoke. Riggs put his small band about and had them assume a line abreast formation astern of the *Salt Lake City*. They were disposed from left to right in the following order: the *Bailey*, *Coghlan*, *Dale*, and *Monaghan*.

At 1147, the signal for course 170° went up the flagship's halyards and two minutes later, course 150°. Another message was flashed off to Kinkaid:

> FOR ACT TO TFC RPT TFC X MY POSIT AT 1115 LAT 53-40 LONG 167-27 X MY COURSE SOUTH X STILL ENGAGED X SEVERAL HITS SLC X SLIGHT DAM X FM CCD1

Four more enemy torpedoes, this time from the *Wakaba*, sped by without hitting. Another shell from the *Salt Lake City* lashed the *Nachi*, this time landing on the right-hand gun of the latter ship's Number I turret. The shell did not detonate, but the violent impact jammed the turret in train. Two Japanese sailors were slain by flying shrapnel.

The brief diversion of her screen had allowed the Japanese a relatively clear view of the *Salt Lake City*. Her list was noted and one account has an 1132 entry that reads, "The enemy

Ken Robinson, executive officer, *Dale.* Courtesy
Ken Robinson

CA began losing oil and fled because of hits by the main
battery of the *Nachi.*" Whether or not this first tangible proof
of damage to the elusive American cruiser raised Japanese
hopes is not mentioned. An entry made at 1150 reads, "All
the enemy ships entered the smoke screen. Their movements
[became] difficult to discern." Even though Fifth Fleet continued in dogged pursuit, Hosogaya was growing increasingly
concerned about the expected arrival of American bombers.[116]

It was at this time that George O'Connell's fears about

119

8-inch ammo consumption came true. Word was passed from the magazine to Bob Matusek that the supply of armor-piercing shot was almost exhausted. He ordered the shell deck to begin sending up high-capacity shells, normally used against unprotected targets, and informed O'Connell of his situation. He also asked if he could fire his drill ammo, a request heard by Ben Johnston. Johnston immediately advised against it, fearing that the oversized drill projectiles would bind in the gun barrels. Several thoughts were going through Matusek's head, as he relates:

> When we began running low on armor-piercing shells, I may have asked about firing drill ammo . . . I guess I probably would have asked permission to throw rocks had the Japs been close enough! I do remember requesting permission to fire only one round at a time to conserve ammo and to keep the morale of the ship's crew up. Seemed to me at the time that the worst thing we could do was to stop firing since we were so low on ammo. In order to conserve armor-piercing ammo, I shifted to high capacitys with the hope that one shell at a time might just possibly cause the Japs to think a plane or two from Amchitka might have gotten over them and was dropping a few bombs. The high capacitys, not having shell dye, just might appear similar to bombs exploding on the water. They did, and the Japs fired off bursts into the overcast.[117]

Matusek's feelings about the effect of the high-capacity shells is supported by fellow turret officer Engle:

> The weather at that time was low overcast. When these shells began to land, the visual effect was quite different from what they had been seeing when the armor-piercing landed—instead of a splash with a dye load which colored the splash, there was a large, black, high order detonation at the water surface. I have always believed, as did others, that this new effect probably convinced them that the air cover we had been radioing for had finally arrived, and that they were under attack by land-based bombers. I also believed that it might have had an effect on their decision to disengage.[118]

Samuel Eliot Morison says nothing, and George O'Connell decries the possibility that the Japanese fired the antiaircraft barrage because of the high-capacity shell bursts. Japanese records make no mention of these larger bursts. However, the *Maya*, and especially the *Nachi*, suddenly let go with a tremendous antiaircraft barrage just after the first of the high-capacity shells landed.[119]

Faced with the prospect that half the ship's main battery would soon be silenced, Jim Brewer's men concocted a desperate remedy: ammunition would be transferred aft. After a hurried conversation between Brewer, O'Connell, and the turret officers, it was decided to shift ammunition from the shell deck of Turret II to the after turrets. A pathway of watertight doors was opened up inside the ship for the passage of the powder cans. The 5-inch and automatic weapon batteries were combed for men to form a passing line. The gunnery repair party was tasked with the job of wheeling the 256-pound shells aft on hand dollies, two men per shell. It was not only an incredible risk, but an incredible feat that the men tackled with a will.

The retelling of the story cannot do justice to the act. It was a task that was conceived, organized, and carried out in a matter of minutes. The ship was under way, heeling to the right or left as Captain Rodgers chased salvos, enemy shells were plunging close aboard, shaking the ship, and the decks were slippery with ice. A hit anywhere along the handling line that was passing the powder through the ship would probably have caused her destruction. Yet nearly 200 rounds were transferred without incident. Worthy Bitler went down to the main deck to witness the transfer and remembers that some of the men actually grinned at him as they wheeled the heavy projectiles aft. Needless to say, the rate of fire of the after turrets was considerably reduced. Matusek writes:

> I know we had to stop firing to train directly aft in order to get the shells below decks to the shell deck. The powder bags

121

were passed by hand from forward aft below decks. After getting a little ammo, we would train out again, fire a few more, then cease firing until we could get some more ammo below decks.[120]

By these makeshift means, the *Salt Lake City* contrived to keep her enemies at bay.

Shorty Dahlen's success in lowering the water level in his engine room now brought him other problems. Just about the time the water level got down to mid-calf level, the big main circulator pump began to race. The water level had fallen so far that there wasn't sufficient water pressure at the suction end for it to work. In addition, great gobs of fuel had to be cleared from the pump intake by someone reaching shoulder deep into the freezing water and scooping the sludge out. After ten or fifteen minutes, the water level was then high enough to again activate the pump. It was an agonizing ordeal for the engineers and the damage controlmen trying to help them. As Dahlen so succinctly states, "Your tutu was frozen!" The word went around among the men that the black streaks showing on their legs and thighs were clots of frozen blood. It later proved to be only fuel oil, but at the time added to their physical and mental anguish.[121]

Other efforts by the black gang to counter the *Salt Lake City's* damage now almost brought her to grief. Just as the gunners were shifting ammo, the engineers were shifting fuel oil in an effort to correct the port list. The after fire room had been shifted to the forward fuel service, and efforts were under way to pump fuel from port to starboard. Perhaps the man was rattled by events; perhaps the unrelenting tension had dulled his attention; perhaps he misunderstood an order. For whatever reason, someone opened the wrong valve and cut all eight of the ship's boilers into a tank ballasted with sea water. White smoke gushed from her stacks at 1150, as all her fires went out. The throttles were wide open, so there was no gradual dying away of steam pressure. The cruiser's propulsive heart was silent in only a minute. Likewise the ship was totally without electrical power, having no emergency diesels as in later classes of cruisers. As if in punctuation of her suddenly extreme plight, two enemy shells blasted into the sea so close aboard the port side that Rodgers was sure his ship had been hit again. All the sensations peculiar to a warship moving at high speed, the rush of the wind over the deck, the sustained roar of air being drawn into fire room intakes, the tremors in the deck as the ship pounds along, the pronounced heel as she turns, all died away as the *Salt Lake City* coasted to a stop on a sea tossed and turn by enemy shellfire. Jim Brewer had asked that the last of her way be used to turn her broadside to the approaching Japanese and this had been done. She now lay rocking gently with the dismal signal, *Mike Speed Zero* fluttering from her yardarm.[122]

In the *Richmond*, meanwhile, Ralph Millsap had returned to the bridge from his battle station in Radio Central. He had taken up a station at the TBS and was relaying messages to McMorris. Beginning at 1153, he began repeating a most distressing sequence of messages from the *Salt Lake City*: "My speed twenty-two. My speed fourteen. My speed eight. My speed four. My speed zero!" At the last report, McMorris made no comment, but according to Millsap, assumed a most unhappy expression. Perhaps he was having the same thoughts that were going through Millsap's mind: "Everyone of us figured, at that point, that this was the end of the battle." Millsap was so convinced of the final outcome that he tried to send a telepathic message of farewell to his wife. Ken Robinson turned to his chief quartermaster and said, "It's not a question of if, it's a question of when." Seaman 2c Larry Norwood, a shell passer on the *Dale*'s Number IV gun, was equally certain that the end was at hand: "I was nineteen at the time. My birthday is April 15. I always wanted to be twenty-one and I didn't think I would make it to twenty." Mike Callahan also thought the game was up: "One of the firecontrolmen turned to me and said, 'Well, I guess it won't be too long now, maybe when they get a little closer we can take a few with us.' I replied,

'You may be right on both counts.' All I could think of was that this was a lonely damn part of the world in which to die."[123]

The feeling that death was imminent was nowhere more pronounced than in the motionless *Salt Lake City*. Worthy Bitler shook hands with Captain Rodgers and quietly said, "Well, I guess this is it." Jim Brewer felt only an overwhelming sense of tiredness. He brought a strained laugh to the men on the bridge when he asked for a cup of coffee. He remarked, "If I'm going into that cold water, I want something warm inside me." With just a tinge of sadness in his gentle Mississippi drawl, Bill Hosey recalls how a calm certitude that he was going to die came over him. With equal quietness, he makes it clear that in no way had he or his men accepted defeat. He did call the engine room to find out the injection temperature. When he was told that the water temperature was 31°, he told his men not to bother with their life jackets. The water was so cold that they had a life expectancy measured in minutes. Seaman 1c Lloyd Webb was a rammerman in Ben Johnston's turret: "I always kept my life jacket stuffed between the sprinkler pipes and the overhead. The force of a near miss was so great that my life jacket fell and hit me. I got the message—I put the life jacket on." In the turret officer's booth, Johnston and his phone talker were having a muted discussion. Some time before, Johnston had the man procure a small wooden keg, which was waterproofed and equipped with cord handles. It was intended to be a last resort float for both of them. As the ship lay motionless, it seemed that the keg would shortly be put to use. Johnston said to the man, "Well, Nick, we're stopped. Shall we flip a coin to see if we go over the port side or the starboard side when we abandon ship?"[124]

Bob Matusek put his life jacket on, took it off, put it on again, and took it off yet again. He was ". . . mad as hell about all the wonderful things I'd be missing." Knowing that survival time in the cold water was very short, he couldn't decide whether to jump over the side or go down with the

Gunner's Mate 2c Lloyd Webb, *front row, far right*, and turret crew, *Salt Lake City*.   Courtesy Lloyd Webb

ship. Bob Taplett wasn't prepared for the end: "When the ship stopped, I just couldn't accept the thought that the ship was lost . . . I'm sure doubt flashed across my mind even though I felt that somehow we would get out of our predicament." The same denial of defeat helped Taplett seven years later when he led his battalion down the long road from Chosin Reservoir. Water Tender 2c Roy Yates remembers that the chief petty officer in his damage control party got up from his seat on the deck, ". . . sorta danced a little jig and said, 'Fellows, up to this time we've kicked the hell out of the Japs but today it looks like they're going to kick the hell out of us.' " Gerry Reeves first told his men to put on their life jackets, but then made it a personal option after considering that rescue was unlikely and death by freezing a near certainty. Since the flooding of the antiaircraft switchboard had wiped out his ability to control the 5-inch guns from the director, he told his gun crews to open fire in local control as soon as the Japanese came into range.[125]

George O'Connell also made preparations for a last-ditch effort:

> I prepared for a last supreme effort. I may have used strong language in telling the turret officers to shoot as they had never shot before; to be prepared to go on order to straight local control. . . . Turrets II and IV were to take the port side, Turrets I and III the starboard. For the time being, we were still in director fire collective, Director II controlling, Spot I spotting.[126]

The preparations being made by the gunners for a last stand were gallant, but they were also contingent upon the word of one man. The captain of a warship is afforded honor and respect, and his authority is as near to absolute as practicable. His responsibility is also nearly absolute, and it is possible for his career to founder on the failings of his most lowly and least-competent subordinate. In the company of 1,200 men, but absolutely alone in his responsibility, Bert Rodgers was faced with the apparent choice of two equally unappealing alternatives—to stay with the ship seemed to offer death under a rain of high-explosive shells. Abandoning the ship offered death by freezing and only the faintest chance of being rescued by the accompanying ships.

Yeoman 1c Bob Drust, a phone talker in company with Rodgers, describes the scene: "I can remember the Captain ordering 'Abandon ship,' then a moment later, 'Belay that last word,' before we had a chance to pass the word through the speaker and phone systems." Drust also remembers Rodgers, ". . . then turning and with a little smile asking if anyone had a piece of gum." It is impossible to know what thoughts ran through Rodgers's mind in those few seconds after his ship came to a stop, but having made his decision, he prepared to sell her dearly. The main battery was ordered to check fire and the transfer of ammo was halted. Stilled generators meant that muscle power now trained the turrets and ran the ammo hoists. The main battery was almost crippled, but Jerry Engle wasn't going without a fight. He told his pointer and trainer, Bosun's Mate 1c Warren Wells and Gunner's Mate 3c Lacy Bennett, "If the Japs come through the smoke screen, pick out the biggest ship in the group and don't miss." Jim Brewer told Rodgers, "We're pretty good in local control, and we can make 'em pay for it when they barrel in on us." It seemed inevitable to the *Salt Lake City*'s men that they were going to have to leave her before the day was much older. Because their captain had decided that a fight, however hopeless, was to be their legacy, they weren't going until the ship was shot to pieces around them.[127]

As bad as the situation looked to the men topside, the most terrifying time was had by the engineers. In the instant before the battle lanterns snapped on, all hands below decks were in total blackness. When the lanterns came on, Vince Dahlen experienced a feeling of seeing a freeze frame in a film: everyone seemed to pause in mid-step, then continue on with his duties. It was an eerie scene about which Dahlen says, "You figure that must have been Hell—you were there!" It was a shadowy, dimly lit Hell which presented Dahlen and his fellow engineers with a seemingly insurmountable problem. The fuel lines had to be purged of seawater, uncontaminated fuel pumped to the boilers, and a draft capable of sustaining boiler fires provided. These were normal procedures, often accomplished. However, they were not usually accomplished under heavy fire, in semi-darkness, without power to drive the pumps and blowers, and with the sure knowledge that the margin for error was nil. Fortunately, the same levelheadedness and individual initiative that conceived and executed the movement of ammo from the forward turrets also made itself felt in the engineering spaces. With Herculean speed and coordination, all hatches leading topside from the fire rooms were flung open. The fuel lines were pumped clear of seawater and fuel pumped to the boilers. With infinite care, for under those conditions it was a task requiring experience and skill, the boilers were refired under a natural draft. The instant steam pressure permitted, generators, and thus, fuel and feed water pumps, were cut in. As air blowers came back on the line, the airlocks were shut and the fire rooms pressurized back to operating level. At 1158, enough steam pressure had built up to turn the turbines. A familiar pulse throbbed through the cruiser's decks as the screws began to move. Life and all its attendant worries was again offered to the men on board the *Salt Lake City*. It is hardly surprising that most of her men feel the restoration of power was little short of miraculous.[128]

THE BATTLE: 1155–1208

While the *Salt Lake City*'s black gang was working miracles, equally desperate efforts were taking place outside the ship. When the signal *Mike Speed Zero* was hoisted to the cruiser's yardarm, her chances of survival seemed dim indeed. Even as she coasted to a stop, a Japanese shell ripped through the *Zero* flag. Six more torpedoes were also swimming toward her, but they were destined to miss. Captain Rodgers had no illusions about what his words meant, but at 1155, he suggested to McMorris that two destroyers attempt a torpedo attack on the enemy. It was a suggestion for which Captain Riggs was already prepared. George Peckham recalls the scene on the *Bailey*'s bridge:

> I recall Captain Riggs saying when the *Salt Lake City* started to slow down, "George, it might be necessary for the destroyers to make a torpedo attack on the Jap heavies to save the *Salt Lake City*. Check with CIC and come up with a torpedo attack course and get the signal ready to hoist." When the *Salt Lake City* said over the TBS, "My speed zero," I distinctly recall that Captain Riggs immediately grabbed the TBS and either suggested to the OTC that the destroyers immediately com-

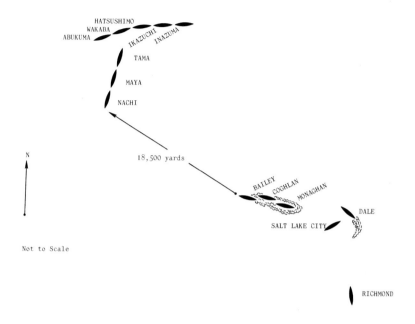

Figure 5. 1157—26 March 1943; torpedo attack by DesRon 14
(*Salt Lake City* dead in water).

mence a torpedo attack on the Jap heavy cruisers or that the
destroyers are commencing a torpedo attack now. On putting
down the TBS, he informed me to hoist the signal for the
torpedo attack. We promptly did, as the signal was already
bent on the hoist waiting to be two-blocked. I did not hear the
OTC's reply over the TBS but I honestly believe that we had
the signal two-blocked before the reply was received.

Ralph Millsap relayed Riggs's message to McMorris, who appeared to mull it over for a moment before he tersely replied,
"Execute."[129]

Riggs directed the *Coghlan* and the *Monaghan* to follow
the *Bailey*. The Japanese were on the *Salt Lake City*'s starboard

129

quarter, so the *Bailey* and *Coghlan* wheeled to the right and reversed course. By the time the *Monaghan* passed down the *Salt Lake City*'s port side and cut across the cruiser's bow, she had fallen some 2,000 yards behind her two squadron mates. The *Dale* was directed to continue shielding the still motionless *Salt Lake City* with smoke. Machinist's Mate 1c Ernie Stahlberg was one of the more than 750 American sailors who were in the ships charging at Fifth Fleet. He was a throttleman in the forward engine room, an old hand who had been on board since 1938. When word of the impending torpedo attack came down, he and the others in the engine room didn't think too much of their chances:

> We were told over the sound-powered phones that we were to make a torpedo attack. Hearing about the numerically superior Japanese force, I felt if we made the attack, we would be very lucky if the ship survived. I just hoped for the best. The Chief came to all stations in the engine room and shook hands with each person and told us how much he had enjoyed serving with us. He also kidded me by telling me that he should have sent me to Diesel School or Sub School as I had requested many times.

Stahlberg adds:

> I had many thoughts of home and my wife who I knew was six months pregnant with our first child and I wondered if I would ever see them.[130]

If Stahlberg and his chief had been topside, they would have felt their fears were justified. Hundreds of splashes were erupting around the *Bailey* and the *Coghlan*. Every gun that the Japanese could bring to bear was firing at the American destroyers. John James describes what it was like aboard the *Coghlan*:

> The shell splashes and explosions looked like Niagara Falls about ten to fifteen feet off the fantail. We were coming in so fast that their fire control problem just never caught up to us.

It looked like forty or fifty shells a second and completely continuous. If their fire control had ever caught up, we'd have been chewed up in seconds.[131]

Undeterred by the storm of steel coming at them, the destroyers plunged on, making smoke and firing as fast as the guns could be served. The *Nachi* was the focal point of much of the destroyer's fire. Several hits were observed and Kintaro Miura later said their shells ". . . landed aboard like rain."[132] Via TBS, Riggs ordered, "Prepare your torpedoes. Target is the big boys."

The attack was an inspirational sight to the cruiser men. Worthy Bitler says the sight of the charging destroyers was the most stirring thing he witnessed in a thirty-year naval career. A Civil War history buff, he says, "Pickett's charge had nothing on them." Gene Purdy was near the TBS speaker on the *Richmond*'s bridge: "The calmness of the destroyer commander's voice on the radio when he brought them to their new course and set up the firing run—you'd think he was going to Sunday school. There wasn't a dry eye on the bridge when they went out of sight." Ben Johnston and Harlan Bumpas were boyhood friends, so when Johnston heard the destroyers were going in against the enemy cruisers, he had the sad thought that he had surely seen the last of his friend.[133]

Almost unbelievably, one man who wasn't too worried was John Atkeson. Since the *Bailey* was in the lead and therefore unable to benefit even minimally from the smoke screen, she naturally bore the brunt of Japanese gunfire. An idea of what was occupying Atkeson's attention can be gained from Frank Ayers's description of the run-in:

> During the torpedo run, we were straddled by Japanese cruisers many, many times. It was a remarkable sight to see an enemy salvo land close aboard a little short. The Captain would turn the ship toward where the salvo had landed and the next salvo would land close aboard a little over. This went on time after time over a period of about ten minutes; then we commenced taking hits. I conclude that Captain Atkeson's expert and in-

tuitive shiphandling, (together with an assist from Providence), saved the ship.[134]

Nevertheless, the *Bailey*'s captain was so intent upon reaching torpedo range that he says no thoughts of losing his ship entered his head. The experiences of Bob Walker and Frank Ayers mirror their captain's:

> [Walker] I really have no recollections about thoughts of losing the ship. I knew when the ship was hit each time, but as I said earlier, when you have a purpose, fear is somehow put into the background. Truly, I cannot give an answer to my thoughts about the *Bailey* surviving the torpedo run.
>
> [Ayers] I was very busy during the torpedo run and communication was very poor (due largely to the almost continuous blast from Number II gun which was firing every three seconds or so). I was too busy to worry, and by the time I ceased to be busy, it was all over. I didn't really think the ship was in danger of being lost until the battle was over and I saw and learned the extent of the damage, found that my roommate was dead, etc. The full realization didn't reach me until weeks later when we were in dry dock at Mare Island.[135]

Hart Kait offers a reflection that might explain, at least in

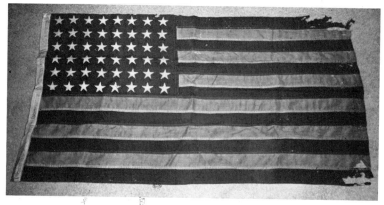

Colors flown over the *Bailey*, 26 March 1943. John Atkeson has had them in his possession since the day of the battle.   Courtesy author

part, the lack of concern on the part of the *Bailey*'s men: "I'd guess that you have to be lost once to get a feeling that you are going to be lost." When questioned about the events of those few furious minutes, a glint of humor appeared in John Atkeson's eyes as he quietly drawled, "I wasn't drinking coffee."[136]

On board the *Nachi*, Kintaro Miura was watching with a mixture of professional admiration and outright incredulity. As he watched the *Bailey* emerge, time and again, from a cluster of shell splashes, the scene was fixed in his memory. More than two and half years later, he told American interrogators, "I do not know how a ship could live through the concentration of fire that was brought to bear on the leading destroyer."[137] The memories of her former crewmen and a former enemy are somber in contrast to the puffery of the *Bailey*'s ship history:

> Closer and closer she went, right into the teeth of the Rising Sun. Crew members even fancied they saw yellow faces peering over the side of the Jap warship—faces displaying no little scorn at the mouse that had dared to threaten the buoyancy of the lion. But *Bailey* was making this a quick trip as she moved in for what she hoped would be the kill.[138]

Reality quickly intervened to dash any unlikely hopes that the *Bailey* was about to make a kill.

The range to the Japanese was down to 10,000 yards when the *Bailey* began to pay the price for her audacity. Shortly after 1200, she was staggered by a blow to the starboard side. A hole described by Harlan Bumpas as being the size of a household door was torn in the ship's side. By an unfortunate twist of fate, the forward damage control party was gathered in the passageway outside the galley. Bumpas had received permission to feed the crew and had mustered the damage control party outside the galley to carry sandwiches and coffee to the men at their battle stations. Bumpas himself was in the galley when the shell struck:

> I had just picked up a dishpan full of ham sandwiches and

133

started out the galley door when I thought that no one had taken care of delivering coffee to the bridge. I turned to the chief standing near me, handed him the dishpan . . . and then turned back into the galley to pick up a tureen of coffee. At that moment, the ship took the hit in the pantry. I was knocked to the deck and was temporarily unconscious. Lights in the whole area were out and it was as black as anything I've ever seen. My first thought was what happened to the chief who was standing just by me. I started calling his name and of course, I got no answer. Immediately I stumbled out the galley door and began hearing the cries and moans of the wounded of which there were many. The rest of the damage control party had been standing or sitting in that passageway just across from the pantry. I later learned that the chief was knocked completely across the galley and was killed. My thoughts of getting coffee to the captain were the probable cause for my being here today.[139]

Eleven men were scythed down by the shell. Four were killed outright and one was mortally wounded. Among the dead was Ensign Ellis Whitehead. He was Frank Ayers's roommate and had joined the ship the day she left Dutch Harbor. A messenger was dispatched to the bridge to report on the damage, and word was passed for the doctor. Those men who were unhurt immediately began plugging the gaping hole in the ship's side and tending to the wounded. The nearby wardroom was turned into an operating room as soon as the doctor arrived. The wounded were placed in officers' bunks and made as comfortable as possible.

Captain Riggs reacted to this hit by ordering Atkeson to get the torpedoes away. The squadron commander was afraid the ship would be disabled before she could get any closer to the enemy. The range of 9,500 yards was asking a lot of the poor American torpedoes, but five of the missiles were sent on their way. As the last one knifed into the water, the ship was hit twice more by shrapnel, this time in both the forward fire room and the forward engine room. It was 1203 and although the exact minute would soon be forgotten, what happened next has remained forever etched in the memories of the men who saw it. To the utter disbelief of all hands, the Japanese started turning away to the west.

The incredulity of everyone is exemplified by the words of one sailor who exclaimed, "Jesus, I don't believe it. They're up to something." It was true, however, and by the time the *Coghlan* came abreast of the *Bailey*, target angle had become too unfavorable to fire torpedoes. No torpedoes were fired by the *Monaghan* either, as she was even farther behind. The retiring Japanese cruisers still managed to smack the *Bailey* once more. In graphic proof of the close range, the shell hit on such a flat trajectory that it only scored a groove in the deck before skittering to a stop. Topside personnel reacted instinctively and rolled the unexploded 8-inch shell over the side. Still another near miss shattered her whaleboat. The following four entries in Atkeson's Action Report are spare in their summation of a terrifying few minutes:

1203 Fired torpedoes. Five expended.
1204 Gyro out, radars out, sound gear out, #1 boiler out of commission.
1207 #1 engine out of commission. All power lost to guns and director. Continued firing in local control.
1209 Speed slowed to 25 knots. Ship vibrating badly.

Frank Ayers didn't think the torpedoes he had fired scored on the enemy, but when several of the *Bailey's* men optimistically reported a hit, he became more hopeful. George Peckham thought the Japanese turned away because the *Nachi* had been hit in the screws by one of the torpedoes. According to Japanese records, four torpedo wakes were spotted. Admiral Mori's chief of staff also said that had it not detonated prematurely, one torpedo would have struck the *Abukuma*.[140]

It is evident from the account of John James that the *Coghlan's* participation in the attack was as memorable to her men as it was to the men of the *Bailey*. One of James's men reacted in a most unexpected way to the news that they were going in against the enemy:

My number-one man was Chief Bosun's Mate Higgins. Higgins had about eighteen years in the Navy. I was still learning things from him and relied on him heavily. I saw Higgins sitting on the tool locker with his head in his hands, mumbling. Everyone was looking at him. My immediate reaction was that I didn't want any panic—fear communicates and spreads. I spoke sharply to Higgins, asking him what was the matter. He looked up at me between his hands and said quite clearly, "I knew it was wrong. I knew it was too good. They gave us that ice cream yesterday [transferred by the *Salt Lake City*], and I had three helpings and now we're going to pay for it. You never get something for nothing in this world!" God, we busted out laughing at this droll Scot humor. Here we are, minutes and seconds from death, and we were all holding our sides laughing. Of course, he did it on purpose!

A minute later, James was on the bridge, where he witnessed Benjamin Tompkins handling the ship:

I guess the only thing I can get across is how utterly capable he was during the torpedo attack. He was standing on the forward part of the bridge, serene and confident, giving quiet orders to the helmsman. He acted and looked like this was just the thing he'd trained his whole career for. He was calm and quiet and acted like fear had never entered his head. He had his orders, had a job to do, and was exercising all of his training and experience to conn the ship . . . into the best position to carry out his mission. A captain can do no more![141]

No direct hits were suffered during the run-in. As the *Coghlan* completed her turn away, an 8-inch shell from the *Maya* hit her foremast and sprayed the bridge with shrapnel. The executive officer and one other man were badly wounded, and her radars were knocked out of commission. As they pulled farther away from the Japanese, the fact that they were going to survive began to sink into her men:

Incredulous!   Unbelieving!   Paltry words for our feelings. Actually, some of us thought it was some kind of trick maneuver—that they were going to come around and get at us some other way after they'd evaded the torpedoes. It wasn't till four or five minutes after they disappeared that it gradually sank in that they were really gone. Someone cracked a joke and said, "I guess we're not going swimming after all."[142]

No one in the *Monaghan* was injured nor did she suffer any damage.

While her squadron mates were heading toward apparent destruction, the *Dale* was faithfully shielding the *Salt Lake City* with smoke. The question being asked aboard both ships was, "Where is the *Richmond?*" McMorris did not react immediately when the *Salt Lake City* slowed to a stop. The wide gulf that developed between the flagship and the center of action caused a good deal of resentment and many vehement assertions by men in both the *Dale* and the *Salt Lake City* that McMorris was leaving the heavy cruiser to her fate. Even the *Richmond's* executive officer was disappointed in the admiral's action:

> When the *Salt Lake City* hoisted the signal, *Mike Speed Zero*, we then had a new ball game—the mainstay of our force crippled. How bad? We didn't know. At that point, I expected and hoped that we would jump back into the fight if for no other reason than to take the heat off the crippled *Salt Lake City*. I am still amazed that we did not. So the fact remains, right or wrong, and for whatever reason, we did not close in and join the fray—we moved away. Again, let me say that I do not know the OTC's overall thinking that culminated in all or even any of his decisions. . . .[143]

John Atkeson, Ralph Millsap, and Al Ovrum feel no good gain could have come of McMorris's putting the flagship within gun range of the Japanese heavy cruisers. They feel the odds were simply too great that the *Richmond* would have suffered serious damage without any hope of inflicting commensurate damage on the enemy. Whether or not her presence any closer to the *Salt Lake City* would have been of any material help is moot. She was an old ship in no way built to take hits from a heavy cruiser. But the fact that the admiral seemed to be keeping her out of harm's way at the time when his force was in its greatest peril is what some of his men remember.[144]

The destroyers were still racing in toward the enemy when the *Salt Lake City* began to move. Captain Rodgers had asked Father Hodge to say a prayer for the ship; as the screws began to bite into the water, Rodgers turned to the priest and exuberantly told him, "Good work, Padre! Now keep that pipeline open!" A cold swim deferred made Jim Brewer very happy: "I had extreme joy when they got that bastard started again." Father Hodge wasn't the only one praying, a fact attested to by Chuck Vasey: "I think everybody on that ship was a converted Christian that day . . . I know I was." Bob Matusek is another one who senses Divine intervention: "The good Lord looked after us on this one. I guess He had other things for us to do." Incredibly, Al Melville and his comrades in the handling room didn't know the ship had been stopped:

> My first recollection of our real situation and that we were in trouble was when . . . the man in the room attached to the magazine opened his door and told us we had been dead in the water. By this time, we were already under way again. "They are quitting. It's all over," was the next thing we heard and that came before we could fully realize what he had told us.[145]

The question that was soon on nearly everyone's lips was why had the Japanese turned away? The enemy had been held at bay throughout the morning chiefly by the long reach of the *Salt Lake City*. When she came to a stop, she became a sitting duck whose loss would have meant the end for the rest of the task group. One sailor feels the enemy turned away because the American destroyers were apparently prepared to commit suicide to save the cruisers. The truth is somewhat more complex. The Japanese were indeed awed by the gallant performance of Riggs's destroyers, but Hosogaya had ordered the turn away before the torpedo attack began. He did so for a variety of reasons: he was discouraged by the lack of ability on the part of his heavy cruisers to score a telling hit, both the *Nachi* and the *Maya* were reporting low supplies of 8-inch ammo, forty-two torpedoes had been fired without a hit, and the destroyers were reporting low fuel states.

The deciding factor was Hosogaya's certainty that American bombers would be on the scene at any minute. He had calculated at the outset of the action that he would have three to four hours breathing space before bombers could be on the scene. That time was exhausted. A message had been received from the naval radar station on Kiska stating that American bombers were en route to the battle area, confirming his fears. Ralph Millsap feels that the Japanese admiral may also have been influenced by an apparent deception played out by the *Salt Lake City*'s radiomen. While at his battle station in *Richmond*'s Radio Central, Millsap was startled to hear a plain language message being transmitted on the Fighter Direction Frequency. The message very clearly related the circumstances of the battle and requested immediate help. From the strength of the signal, Millsap surmised that it could only come from the *Salt Lake City*. He suggests that since American forces monitored Japanese circuits, there is no reason to believe the Japanese didn't do the same. It is a speculative theory, but the Japanese did say that the turn away was partially prompted by radio intelligence concerning the arrival of American bombers.[146]

What Samuel Eliot Morison chose to overlook and McMorris chose not to agree with, is that even before the *Salt Lake City* was stopped, the range to the Japanese was opening. The following table was compiled in the *Salt Lake City*'s CIC:

Time	Range to Enemy
1150	23,000 yards
1151	22,750 "
1152	22,250 "
1153	22,750 "
1154	23,250 "
1155	23,375 "
1156	23,500 "
1157	24,000 "

There is no reason to believe that this table does not reflect the actual course of events. Howard Grahn was controlling the battery when the ship went dead in the water. He was

139

fully expecting the Japanese to come charging through the smoke and deluge the ship with close-range gunfire. It took a minute for the realization to dawn on him that the ranges being called out by the rangefinder operator were opening ranges. He thought to himself, "Opening? My God, how can it be opening?"[147] For the most significant reason of many, the range *was* opening. Admiral Hosogaya had given up the fight. What had appeared to be an easy victory four hours before had proved to be a fight demanding a greater price than the Japanese admiral was willing to pay. The gallantry of the American destroyermen is in no way lessened by the fact that they were attacking a man who had already admitted defeat.

The exhilarating sense of deliverance being felt in the *Salt Lake City* and the returning destroyers was mirrored in the *Dale*. Ken Robinson was jubilant: "That was the happiest day of my life. That was the best medal I ever had." Mike Callahan was doubting what his eyes were telling him: "When I observed the Japanese ships turning away, I simply did not trust my eyes. Our normally very quiet stereo rangefinder operator let out a yell as well as the signalmen on the bridge." Not only had the task group survived, but they were sure they had sent the enemy skulking home with his tail between his legs.[148]

At 1204, Fifth Fleet's parting shots splashed into the sea around the *Salt Lake City*. At 1208, she fired her last shots of the battle. The Japanese were headed for the western horizon and would soon be out of sight. Captain Riggs radioed the task group commander wanting to know if the destroyers should follow the enemy, but McMorris told them to rejoin the formation. The gallant *Bailey* would not have been able to follow too far because she was having a hard time with her damage. The six-inch hole in the forward fire room had been plugged, but the twenty-inch hole in the forward engine room was behind a pump and therefore inaccessible to shoring. Fortunately, John Atkeson was as well served by his subordinates as Bertram Rodgers. Atkeson's engineering officer, Lieutenant Ralph Moreau, records his reaction to the danger:

> I might mention one experience that surprised me and which I never before experienced. When we took a waterline hit . . . and water spray was seemingly everywhere, to me, everything went into slow motion. I was able to think clearly, make decisions, issue orders with plenty of time to spare, all in the face of great fear.

As in the *Salt Lake City*, the main circulator pump was put to work as a bilge pump. Unfortunately, the oil supply to the pump began to fail. When a standby oil pump also failed, the forward engine room had to be abandoned. The steady flow of damage reports to the bridge could be heard at several stations, giving rise to rumors that the ship was sinking. Men in the magazines and other below-decks stations began to mentally measure the distance to the nearest escape scuttle. They need not have worried, for the *Bailey* was not destined to sink. She followed her sisters back toward the *Salt Lake City* at 24 knots, all she could manage on one engine.[149]

CHAPTER 3

Retirement and Aftermath

Ironically, as tension began to drain away from Mc-Morris's men, some worrisome messages were being put into Admiral Kinkaid's hands. Shortly after 1200, he received one that read:

FOR ACTION TO CTF RPT CTF 16 X SALT LAKE CITY SPEED REDUCED TO 20 KNOTS

Minutes later, another, more ominous message was handed to him:

SALT LAKE CITY STOPPED REPEAT STOPPED X DALE STANDING BY X OUR DDS ATTACK-ING X FROM CCD1 TO TFC RPT TFC

Any fears Kinkaid may have experienced must have been greatly eased by McMorris's 1223 message:

CTF 16 FROM CCD1 X SALT LAKE NOW MAK-ING 22 MY POSIT 53-10 LONG 167-30 X MY COURSE EAST X ENEMY TO WESTWARD

At 1224, McMorris ordered course 090° and reduced task force speed to 20 knots. In the struggling *Bailey*, steam and vapor suddenly filled the after fire room. The main feed pumps had to be secured and at 1230, the ship went dead in the water. Benjamin Tompkins brought the *Coghlan* about and ordered towing gear broken out. It was never put to use as Ralph Moreau's fast-working black gang took only four minutes to get the ship under way again. In order not to leave the two destroyers too far behind, the rest of the task group had meanwhile slowed to 15 knots. Until the *Bailey* could get her radios back into operation, the *Coghlan* remained in close company to act as a relay ship.

At 1251, an unidentified radar contact gave rise to fears that the Japanese were returning. The morning's adventures must not have been enough for one man on the *Richmond*, because he yelled to his comrades, "Them [sic] Japs are coming back. Let's kick the hell out of them." To the great relief of everyone else, it proved to be a false contact. When it became evident that the enemy was not coming back, all ships unloaded their guns through the muzzle. Ralph Moreau had the *Bailey*'s depth charges jettisoned in an effort to lighten ship. His black gang was also busy transferring fuel in an effort to counter the free surface effect of the flooded fire and engine rooms. In midafternoon, the ships of the task group began to secure from general quarters. Peter Gaviglio chanced upon McMorris just outside the admiral's sea cabin. Gaviglio congratulated McMorris on his performance and received a tired smile in reply. The after sections of the destroyers and the *Salt Lake City* were heavily coated with the sooty residue resulting from nearly two hours of making smoke. One man with a topside station remembers that he and his shipmates looked like actors in blackface.[150]

In the *Monaghan*, a furious Dick Graffius went directly from his seat in the director to the bridge. Oblivious to the rules, he confronted Peter Horn about the alleged shirker in the director: "I told him what happened and that it would be a good idea if he transferred _____ or myself before I killed him. The Captain didn't say anything but we weren't in port long before _____ had his sea bag and orders for transfer on the quarter deck." In the *Dale*, Ken Robinson's first order of business was seeing to the feeding of the crew. The men barely had time to start swapping stories when the general alarm sounded again. At 1604, aircraft were seen approaching from the east. Nervous and tired gun crews made ready to open fire, but the aircraft were identified as American Army bombers. The long anticipated help had arrived, though far too late. Guided by a PBY that had arrived earlier, the Army fliers headed west. To the great disgust of the Navy men, the bombers soon returned, radioing that the enemy ships were out of range. Another group of bombers showed up an hour later, but they also turned back without attacking. This performance did not endear the Army Air Force to the sailors of Task Group 16.6. Months later, some Army fliers in Hawaii would find themselves dazed and bruised and wondering just what the hell they had done to offend those sailors from the USS *Salt Lake City*.[151]

McMorris ordered the *Salt Lake City* and the *Bailey* to return to Adak and advised Kinkaid that he intended to patrol off Holtz Bay, Attu, in the event the Japanese tried to slip the transports in under the cover of darkness. Kinkaid decided that enough was enough and ordered the entire task group to return to base. As battle tension drained away, a protective sense of numbness descended on the men. Ben Johnston went into the wardroom where the casualties were still being attended to. He was so dulled with fatigue that the sight of blood had no effect on him. What did bother him was the sight of Windsor Gale's body, which was still lying in the passageway outside the wardroom. Johnston dazedly thought, "Why are they leaving him here and why do I have to keep stepping over him? He was a friend of mine and I don't want to step over him." Captain Rodgers ordered the doctor to supply all hands with a liberal shot of medicinal alcohol. Johnston turned his down even though he says he was not one to turn down a drink.[152]

Since the ship was holed below the waterline, there was no way to dewater the flooded shaft alleys until the outer hole was patched. Water continued to seep into the after engine room, requiring constant use of the pumps. The problem posed by the cold-thickened oil clogging the pump intake screens was solved by rigging live steam heads at the pump intakes to melt the oil. A constant watch also had to be maintained on the shored-up laundry room bulkhead. Sand had been spread to combat the oil slick on the deck, but the wedges still tended to work loose with the movement of the ship. Topside, over 700 rounds of 40-mm ammunition had to be jettisoned from the fantail mounts. It had been blast damaged to such an extent that it was considered unserviceable.[153]

More than one of the *Salt Lake City*'s sailors stopped to stare at her 8-inch guns. Blistered and flaking paint on all ten barrels gave mute testimony to the battle. The tube liners of Turret III's guns protruded from the muzzles nearly an inch. Hundreds of small pieces of shrapnel littered the decks. Late in the day, the task group received a message from Fleet Headquarters in Pearl Harbor that ended:

YOUR JUDGEMENT AND COURAGEOUS ACTION APPROVED IN EVERY RESPECT. NIMITZ

It was only one of a spate of messages that were passing between the flagship, the destroyers, and the *Salt Lake City*. One message of thanks was addressed to Ralph Riggs and his destroyermen:

THE SLC EXTENDS ITS HEARTFELT THANKS FOR THE MAGNIFICENT WORK YOU AND YOUR BOYS DID TODAY X WE ARE PROUD OF YOU AND DAMNED GRATEFUL

Around 2200 that night, Fireman David gave up the struggle and succumbed to his wounds. Lieutenant Commander David Hawkins, the *Salt Lake City*'s navigator, made a final entry in her Deck Log for 26 March 1943: "This day the hand of Divine Providence lay over the ship. Never before in her colorful history has Death been so close for so long a time. The entire crew offered its thanks to Almighty God for His mercy and protection."[154]

Efforts to dewater the ship began in earnest on the 27th. Submersible pumps were successfully used up to a point. As the water level in the flooded compartments fell, oil and water congealed into a mass that became impervious to pumping efforts. Bucket brigades were pressed into action, work that Seaman 1c Jim O'Hara remembers as back-breaking. The laundry had to be cleared almost entirely by buckets as loose clothing made pumping of any sort impossible. The most hazardous task was clearing the after 5-inch magazine. Gerry Reeves witnessed that operation:

> It was necessary to bring up the hundreds of 5-inch shells from the flooded magazine. They were carried up manually, one at a time, by tired sailors, slipping and falling in the greasy mess. Upon arrival topside, each shell was removed from its case, bathed in hot, soapy water, and . . . stacked topside. Since the weather was freezing, the crew exhausted, the decks like greased ice, and since each shell had a live primer in its base which needed only a . . . blow to cause an explosion which would have wiped out the entire topside aft, this was probably a more dangerous period than many parts of the main engagement. Fortunately, it was accomplished without incident.[155]

Almost without incident, as related by Bob Drust:

> I could see men working in the messhall stacking ammunition there from the ammunition rooms that had ruptured bulkheads. I was sitting at a desk in the office talking to one of the ship's bakers who had dropped by when we heard the word passed, "Fire in the messhall." Upon realizing what was said, [the baker] took off out of the office at a dead run. For some reason, I just sat there thinking that if there was a fire, the ammunition would explode and the ship would sink so why bother to run?[156]

Fortunately, there was no fire.

Of the other ships, only the *Bailey* had to cope with serious damage, and most bothersome to her men was the loss of the

Escutcheon of the *Salt Lake City*, designed by Worthy
Bitler. Courtesy author

galley. They had to subsist on crackers, sandwiches, and whatever other dry goods the cooks could scrounge up. As he
examined the wreckage of the galley, John Atkeson quietly
thought to himself, "Well, there goes my chow."[157] The guns
were hardly stilled when McMorris ordered his captains to
submit their Action Reports. Before the *Salt Lake City* detached

148

ESCUTCHEON OF THE U.S.S. SALT LAKE CITY

REPRESENTATION

1. LOYALTY TO AND DEFENSE OF THE UNITED STATES (REPRESENTED BY THE STARS AND STRIPES)

2. THE SWORD OF DEFENSE WITH THE WREATH OF VICTORY

3. THE MOTTO (NEVER UNPREPARED)

4. THE SHIELD WITH THE CROSS OF CHRISTIANITY AND FREEDOM

5. DEFENSE OF OUR COUNTRY ON THE LAND, THE SEA, AND IN THE SKIES. (REPRESENTED BY THE SEA, TRIDENT AND GULLS UPPER LEFT, THE SKIES UPPER RIGHT, LOWER LEFT SHOWING THE GREAT DIPPER AND THE NORTH STAR, AND THE SOUTHERN CROSS; THE LAND SHOWING, MOUNTAINS, FIELDS AND TREES.)

Representation of the *Salt Lake City*'s escutcheon. Courtesy author

from the task group for Dutch Harbor on the 27th, Rodgers sent this message to the admiral:

AM PREPARING LIST OF DAMAGE FOR YOUR REPORT WHICH WILL FOLLOW MY SIGNAL X PRELIMINARY BATTLE REPORT WILL NOT BE READY IN SMOOTH TODAY X RECOMMEND

YOU SEND DD TO SALT LAKE CITY JUST BE-
FORE DARK TO RECEIVE DATA AND TRACK
CHART IN ROUGH X IT SEEMS EASIER TO
FIGHT THESE THINGS THAN TO WRITE
ABOUT THEM

The truth of David Hawkins's entry in the ship's log was
much in evidence on Sunday, 28 March. Father Hodge held
Divine Services to such an overflow crowd that he had to
repeat the service. One man who was there writes:

> It took quite a while to realize just how close we came to meeting
> up with the Boss. I guess Sunday morning when Father Hodge
> said Mass you really got the message. It was in the mess hall
> and it was jam packed. You could not get another body in
> there. On an ordinary Sunday, we would have twenty or twenty-
> five show up for Mass. Shows what a scare can do to a person.[158]

Later that same day, the *Richmond*, the *Bailey*, and the *Dale*
pulled into Kuluk Bay, Adak. The bodies of Ensign Whitehead
and the other men killed were removed from the *Bailey* soon
after she anchored. The three men requiring hospitalization
were also transferred ashore. The ships in company with the
Bailey half-masted their colors in honor of her dead. Harlan
Bumpas had meanwhile learned that the *Salt Lake City* had
suffered some casualties, but could get no other information.
He worried about his boyhood friend.

The three other ships of the task group went directly to
Dutch Harbor, where they arrived on the morning of the 29th.
As soon as the *Salt Lake City* was moored, she, too, sent her
hospital cases ashore. The next morning Captain Rodgers,
Worthy Bitler, twenty-five officers, and 143 sailors left the
ship to perform a sad duty. A biting wind pulled and tugged
at the Colors as the shoulder-borne coffins of Lieutenant Commander Gale and Fireman David were carried to the military
cemetery. As Father Hodge read the burial service, the ship
that had been their temporary home half-masted her colors.
When the words were finished, an Army honor guard crashed

Father Hodge reading the burial service for LCDR Gale and Fireman David, both killed 26 March 1943.   Courtesy Worthy Bitler

out a volley, and the two Navy men were committed to the cold ground of Alaska.

While in Dutch Harbor, the *Salt Lake City* was deliberately listed to starboard to expose the hole in her port side. A temporary cofferdam was put into place, and after it was pumped dry, a patch was welded over the hole. While this was taking place, the *Bailey* and the *Dale* pulled in from Adak. Their officers and men quickly found out what had already been discovered by their comrades in the *Coghlan* and *Monaghan*: destroyer sailors were tops to the crew of the *Salt Lake City*. John James writes:

> About midmorning, I went . . . aboard the *Salt Lake City* to see her battle damage and talk to some of their officers about the battle from their point of view. Very much the young, bushy-tailed professional naval officer! I was utterly amazed to

151

find out we were blooming heroes! I was told by the Executive Officer to get word back to the ship that everything on the *Salt Lake City* was open to destroyer sailors: clothing from small stores, anything in the canteen, the soda fountain was open— and it was all free! Nothing was too good for destroyer sailors aboard the *Salt Lake City*.[159]

Ed Brown wrote as part of a diary entry for 29 March, "Every time we go over on the S.L. they give us anything we want." The outpouring of appreciation culminated in a tremendous beer bash thrown by the *Salt Lake City* for the destroyermen. It was a riotous affair. Chuck Vasey witnessed at least one boat load of his shipmates being hoisted back into the ship in a cargo net. All hands considered the ship's funds well spent. The destroyermen unanimously described it as a "hell of a party." They were particularly pleased with the gallons and gallons of ice cream provided to them by the *Salt Lake City*. Ben Johnston and Harlan Bumpas passed the evening in the Officer's Club swapping old stories and quietly thanking the Lord for their escape. Celebration and temporary repairs completed, the *Salt Lake City* and the *Bailey* headed south for the warmer climes of California and dock yard hands.[160]

As soon as both ships arrived at Mare Island, they were dry-docked and work began to restore them to duty. Frank Ayers was one of the many men who went down into the dry dock to inspect his ship:

> I saw the hull of the ship dented, wrinkled, and bent for many, many feet where enemy 8-inch shells had exploded close aboard. It is a miracle we weren't sunk. The account of the battle . . . stated that a good third of the *Bailey*'s underwater plates were wrinkled and dented from near misses. Whether it was a third of the plates or not, I was appalled at the extent of the damage and was grateful to be alive.[161]

On a more mundane level, Jim O'Hara remembers the astonishment he felt when a supply officer at Mare Island tried to lower his claim for clothing loss in the flooding. He does admit

Ben Johnston holding the escutcheon of the *Salt Lake City*, May 1981.   Courtesy author

that he eventually settled for 50 percent. Soon after the cruiser arrived in California, Rodgers was summoned to Washington by his old boss, Admiral King, to give a personal account of the battle. As a result of his story and McMorris's report, an investigation was launched to find out why Army air support had been so late in arriving. According to the subsequent Army report, the contact report arrived when all the bombers on Adak had already been bombed up for a strike on Kiska. The general-purpose bombs they carried were deemed unsuitable for attacking warships, so the bombers had to be rearmed. By the time they were reloaded with armor-piercing bombs, Hosogaya was almost out of danger. The Army argument may have been technically correct, but the Japanese admiral was so leery of American airpower that the appearance of bombers over his fleet would have made him break off much sooner. The tardy appearance of the Army airmen didn't make them many friends among the Navy men, but at least one sailor philosophically observed that ". . . the Army always gets lost over water."[162]

In the course of the inevitable summing up, McMorris came in for a smattering of official criticism for accepting the fight and for not launching his spotting planes. If for anything, McMorris should be faulted for overconfidence and lack of pre-action planning. There is nothing in McMorris's actions or subsequent reports to indicate that he ever questioned the intelligence data he received. Lulled by *Ultra*, McMorris approached the morning of 26 March overconfident in his expectations of encountering only lightly escorted merchantmen. The unexpected appearance of the *Nachi* and the *Maya* gave him no choice but flight.

McMorris's overconfidence is also exemplified by his lack of pre-action planning. Nowhere in the memories of the participants or in his Action Report is there any indication that McMorris planned for anything other than a walkover of some transports. In fairness to him, his task force was constituted at sea, and bad weather forestalled any exercises he may have planned. There is no evidence, however, that McMorris communicated with his captains about tactics to be employed, the role of any ship, or what he planned should enemy men-o-war be encountered. Jerry Miller is one who feels the nature of the action may have been different if McMorris had been more farsighted:

> It's very, very obvious that had the admiral been tuned to aviation, with the good intelligence information that he had, the first thing he should have planned on doing was, at first light, to have launched those aircraft, got them in the air, and got a good picture on it. Had he done that, he would have known well ahead of time what the composition of the [enemy] force was. He could have regrouped his force, gotten in a different position, and we would never have had all those lives threatened. The first thing you want out is your scout. That's what those airplanes were for.[163]

The words of McMorris's Action Report, which portray him as considering several alternative courses of action, are no more than a natural effort to put the best possible light on what he did, and, in fact, they do. Given the post he received subsequent to the Komandorski action, McMorris's superiors couldn't have been too displeased. The relatively small amount of damage suffered by his ships and the fact that the Japanese resupply effort was thwarted no doubt helped his case.

More scathing was the criticism level at him by personnel of the *Salt Lake City* and the *Dale*. The few minutes that the *Salt Lake City* was dead in the water were desperate moments for many men. As topside personnel in both ships watched the *Richmond* pull ever farther away, an unshakable conviction that the admiral was leaving them to their fate was born. Jerry Miller remembers the animosity that arose: "There was a general feeling that we were not heroes of that action. The *Richmond* was known as the 'Greyhound of the Pacific.' " Although Miller says of McMorris, "All my life I've thought . . . of him as the guy who saved our skins in the Komandorski action," he also says, "I would like to think that had I been the admiral, I wouldn't have been out there that far away in the first place."[164]

Again, whether the *Richmond*'s presence any closer to the other ships would have been of any aid is moot. The fact remains that McMorris allowed his flagship to stand off a good distance before returning to the center of action, and that is what the men remember. For some, the animosity born in 1943 is still alive.

Less impassioned, but still critical, comments are made by some of the *Salt Lake City*'s officers. They feel that their ship should have been allowed to open fire long before she was, thereby taking advantage of her long reach. Ben Johnston very heatedly says, "The book I read says the guy that opens fire first has the best chance of winning the battle." Opinion is divided about the westward course chosen by McMorris, but being able to fight only half the ship's main battery remains an irritating frustration. Worthy Bitler writes: "In *my opinion*, [Bitler's emphasis], had Captain Rodgers or Captain Riggs been OTC, we would have attacked instead of fighting a retiring action . . . at extreme ranges."[165]

The successful extrication of McMorris's task group from the trap in which they found themselves can be credited to five things: the efficacious use of smoke and the gallant attack by the destroyers, a phenomenal streak of good luck, the wise decision on the part of McMorris to give Rodgers the freedom to maneuver his ship, and the sterling performance by the officers and men of the *Salt Lake City*. Ralph Riggs's adroit handling of his destroyers kept the maximum amount of smoke possible between the *Salt Lake City* and the enemy. It was a performance that won the professional admiration of the Japanese and was mentioned in postwar interrogations. The daring torpedo attack also won Japanese admiration and was probably what McMorris had in mind when he wrote these words in his Action Report: "When the going is tough, the enemy may not know it, and be so concerned over his own troubles that an aggressive act will deter him from pressing you."[166]

To Jerry Miller, luck was *the* most important thing:

The nature of warfare is that you can never give up in any

kind of a combat situation. You just stick with it until you're dead. That's all there is to it. You never know what the other guy's going to do. You just stick with it and eventually luck will take care of you. That's really what happened in this.

No American who was there that day will deny that luck played a part in the day's events, least of all Bertram Rodgers. But as Jim Brewer points out, luck often goes hand in hand with good performance. It is Brewer's opinion, as well as that of many others, that Rodgers was lucky because he was a superior naval officer. On that morning so many years ago, Rodgers was new to his ship, new to his officers, and under fire for the first time. Yet so cannily did he maneuver his ship and by extension, the whole task group, that the enemy managed only five direct hits. It was a performance that is no less impressive more than forty years after the fact.[167]

The final factor in the escape of Task Group 16.6 is the performance of the crew of the *Salt Lake City*. Her men overcame every sort of problem faced by a warship in combat. Her gunners kept the Japanese under accurate fire despite several severe mechanical failures in their equipment. Her engineers and damage control personnel overcame problems that could easily have resulted in her loss. The seeming invulnerability generated by this performance aggravated Hosogaya's uncertainties and ultimately contributed to his decision to break away. Nothing can detract from the performance of the other American ships, but the clearly outstanding performance of the *Salt Lake City* was the reason all survived to fight another day.

Naturally enough, the crew of the *Salt Lake City* are extremely proud of their captain. In 1981, Bertram Rodgers was a very elderly man, but when asked about the battle, some of the fire and excitement of that day came into his voice. Nonetheless, he disdained the notion that his actions were in any way heroic: "I didn't do a damn thing. I had a whole crew there that was doing things for me." He admitted that "Everybody was delighted with the outcome, including me the most."

At least two officers outside of the *Salt Lake City* feel Rodgers was the leading personality of the battle. Mike Callahan writes:

> In talking to bridge personnel after the battle, and later, while listening to the voice radio when I had the deck as we were retiring, I believe the CO of the *Salt Lake City* was the real leader in the battle. He made many suggestions concerning tactics and twice I heard Admiral McMorris call him on the voice radio and thank him for his contributions during the fight.

John James has similar recollections:

> The really magnificent thing that day was the way Bertram Rodgers handled things. He fought his ship beautifully and from our lowly point of view, seemed to take charge of the task group. He was, however, punctilious in the way he executed. For instance: TBS message to flag suggesting a thirty-degree change in the battle line axis to the south. . . . Flag responds to make it so, etc., etc. This sort of thing went on all morning.

It is to McMorris's credit that he was willing to accept guidance and advice from an officer junior to himself. It not only saved the day for his task group, but might have saved his life. The interception of D Convoy didn't work out as planned for either side. However, since the Japanese transports never reached Attu, the Americans must be adjudged to have accomplished their mission. Since Attu was invaded by the Americans not too long after the Komandorski fight, the toll in blood for both sides was made somewhat lower by Hosogaya's failure to land the reinforcements in D Convoy.[168]

The Navy followed its usual policy about releasing news of a battle. A communiqué was issued by the Navy Department in Washington on 28 March, but it was not until 5 May that any substantive details appeared in American newspapers. Even then, the names of the ships were withheld. Two war correspondents had been with the task group, one aboard the *Richmond* and the other aboard the *Salt Lake City*. William Worden's story was in keeping with the times: the battle was made to appear a rout of the Japanese and the supposed total of enemy ships is in error. John Bishop's dramatic story appeared in the 5 February 1944 *Saturday Evening Post*. It is entitled "My Speed Zero," and it appears that every man who served in the *Salt Lake City* bought a copy. The San Francisco News also printed a short article in which Frank Ayers and three of his shipmates are pictured, but again, no ships' names are mentioned. The new officer who had such a bad time when he first joined the *Richmond* fictionalized the Komandorski battle in a work entitled *The Deep Six*. A movie of the same name starring Alan Ladd and William Bendix was also produced.

In June 1943, the battle was refought on the game board of the Naval War College. Bertram Rodgers obviously had a premonition of the outcome when he included the following comments in his Action Report of three months earlier:

> It is realized that the interception at Komandorski Islands will not work out on a game board; but it will work out in fact. While this ship did all in her power to fight effectively and take advantage of each opportunity, it is fully appreciated and humbly acknowledged that only the will of Divine Providence saw our forces through on that day.

His premonition was accurate, for after fifty-one moves on the game board, the following results were adjudged to have occurred:

RESULTS OF THE NAVAL WAR COLLEGE REPLAY OF THE BATTLE OF THE KOMANDORSKI ISLANDS

Ship	*% Damage*
Maya	15
Nachi	13
Tama	93
Abukuma	12
Richmond	10
Salt Lake City	95
Bailey	6
Dale	1

According to the theoretical outcome, both the *Tama* and the *Salt Lake City* were finished. Those sailors of both sides who are alive today would no doubt be unwilling to trade the theoretical outcome for the real, despite the terrors incumbent in the latter.[169]

McMorris soon left the North Pacific. He became Admiral Nimitz's chief of staff in May 1943, a position he held until the end of the war. He received the Distinguished Service Medal for the Komandorski fight. He retired a vice admiral and died in 1954 while in Valparaiso, Chile. A man of strong passions, his supporters are firmly behind him, while his detractors are just as firmly against him. Bertram Rodgers was awarded the Navy Cross for the Komandorski action. He later served with Lord Mountbatten for six months and commanded an amphibious group in the invasion of Southern France. His command was then transferred back to the Pacific, where he participated in the invasions of Iwo Jima and Okinawa. They were training for the proposed invasion of Japan when the war ended. He retired from the Navy as a vice admiral and died in November 1983. Ralph Riggs also received a Navy Cross, though Rodgers jokingly told him he should have a lifesaving medal instead. Riggs later commanded the battleship *South Dakota* and ended the war in command of a cruiser division. Vice Admiral Riggs died in April 1981. Captain Waldschmidt received the Legion of Merit for the Komandorski action; he died in 1972. John Atkeson received the Navy Cross and ended the war in command of Destroyer Division 20. He was the last skipper of the *New Jersey* prior to her Vietnam-era recommissioning. He retired a rear admiral and lives in Norfolk, Virginia. The other three destroyer captains were awarded Silver Star medals and all three retired as rear admirals. Only Benjamin Tompkins survives.

Worthy Bitler and Jim Brewer received Silver Stars and also retired as rear admirals. Both are elderly men, but remain vigorously alert and have vivid memories of that day in the North Pacific. Their pride in the *Salt Lake City* is still evident these many years later. Worthy Bitler lives in New Jersey and Jim Brewer in rural New Hampshire. Vince Dahlen and Bob Matusek received Silver Stars and retired from the Navy with the rank of commander. Vince Dahlen races a gleaming yellow dune buggy across the wastes of Baja California for relaxation. Ben Johnston received the Bronze Star and retired from the Navy as a captain. He is a gracious host, a gentlemen without peer, and has endured hours of interrogation about the battle without complaint. He has an excellent memory, which appears to have retained everything he ever learned about naval gunnery. He lives in Saratoga, California. Chuck Vasey also lives in Saratoga. He later gained a commission and retired from the Navy as a commander (SC). He had the unusual experience of being recalled to active duty for three years during the Vietnam war. Father Hodge remained in the Naval Reserve until 1964, retiring with the rank of commander. Until recently he lived in Santa Cruz, just over the hill from Ben Johnston and Chuck Vasey. He is quite a story teller and remains in contact with many of the men with whom he served. Ken Robinson retired as a captain and lives in Severna Park, Maryland. He is a font of information about the prewar Navy, destroyers, life in the Aleutians, and particularly about that one frightening morning. Ralph Millsap left the Navy after the war, but put in twenty years as a reservist and retired as a commander. He lives in Gleneden Beach, along the lush Oregon coast. He puts his case for the *Richmond* quietly, but with a firm, no-nonsense determination. As may be expected, a fine picture of the *Richmond* hangs on the wall of his study.

Hosogaya was far less fortunate than his American counterpart. His superiors were dismayed by his failure to destroy the American task group. He was involuntarily placed on the retired list in July 1943. He died in 1964 at the age of eighty. Hosogaya truly did have a force strong enough to destroy the Americans. He had overwhelming superiority of gunpower, he had a speed advantage, and he had superiority of numbers. Nevertheless, he chose first to defend his transports and then

Rodgers pins the Silver Star medal on LT(jg) Vince "Shorty" Dahlen.   Courtesy Vince Dahlen

to play a waiting game. Had he displayed any aggressiveness of note, the outcome may well have been in his favor. In his defense, it must be recognized that his air spotter plane, which theoretically gave him an advantage, performed abysmally. The airmen saw that the *Salt Lake City* was stopped, but made no report until they landed at Attu. His destroyers also per-

162

LT Jim Mew received his Silver Star at the same time.   Courtesy
Vince Dahlen

formed poorly, showing nothing of the usual elan of Japanese
destroyermen. A measure of the American's good luck and
Hosogaya's lack of luck is found in the fact that forty-two
torpedoes were fired by the Japanese and none struck home.
The outcome of the battle would surely have been different
had even one of those devastating weapons hit.

RETIREMENT AND AFTERMATH

Only the Japanese flagship required extensive repairs. Not only did the *Salt Lake City* hit her, but also many 5-inch hits were scored by the American destroyers as they charged in on their torpedo attack. There are varying accounts of her loss of personnel: Samuel Eliot Morison cites Kintaro Miura's assertion that a 5-inch shell passed through the gun port of the *Nachi*'s Number I turret and killed the turret crew. As the range to the *Nachi* at the time of the alleged hit was far outside even the maximum range of the American destroyers, this report can't be true. A second report that says the *Nachi* suffered twenty-seven dead seems more likely.[170] While the *Salt Lake City* was resting on dry-dock blocks at Mare Island Navy Yard, the *Nachi* was likewise reposing in Sasebo Navy Yard. None of the other Japanese ships engaged was seriously damaged. Of the eight ships with Hosogaya on 26 March, none survived the war. Their twisted wreckage lies rusting and scattered across the Western Pacific. Each fell victim to the onslaught of the United States Navy that eventually ended in Tokyo Bay.

Of the American ships, only the *Monaghan* didn't survive the war. She capsized in the great typhoon of December 1944, leaving only six survivors. Many men who witnessed the Komandorski fight went down with her. The other three of the "Four Irishmen" who were with McMorris that morning were all decommissioned in 1946. Both the *Bailey* and the *Coghlan* survived on the Naval Vessel Register until 1968 and 1971, respectively. Old and worn out, the *Richmond* was decommissioned in 1945 and scrapped in 1946. Equally worn out, the *Salt Lake City* was kept around long enough to serve in Operation Magic Carpet, and then she, too, was decommissioned in 1946. The first of many, she was out of date and no longer wanted. Along with several other veteran ships and some of her former enemies, she was used as a moored target during the Bikini atom bomb tests. The blast did not sink her, but both funnels were toppled. She was eventually towed back to the United States, a radioactive hulk. Her ignominious end came in May 1948, when she was bombed and shelled by ships and aircraft of the Navy she had served so well. After five hours of this unkind treatment, the submarine *Blenny* was called in to deliver the final blow. As the pillar of water raised by the torpedo subsided, the *Salt Lake City* could be seen heeling to port. Battered and disfigured, her slim hull rent and torn, she went to her grave bow first. Vince Dahlen was there at the finish, watching from the deck of one of her successors. As he watched his old ship roll over and sink, he cried out to no one in particular, "Dammit, somebody half-mast the colors." It was also reported that as her stern disappeared beneath the waves, a commemorative plaque fell off the wall of the Naval Science Building of the University of Utah in Salt Lake City. The spirit of this pioneer ship lives on, though. Her former crewmen have held six reunions, the latest taking place in the summer of 1983. None of the other ships engaged that day can match that record.[171]

The Battle of the Komandorski Islands became history more than forty years ago. Many of the men who fought there died in the victorious push across the Pacific. Many others have died in the intervening years. The young sailors and junior officers have already or are now retiring from their post-Navy careers. Yet the battle remains indelibly etched in their memories. Dick Graffius is one of those for whom the memories are very real: "It's funny now, but . . . I haven't forgotten after nearly forty years. This battle was much worse than 7 December 1941 because of the duration and what appeared to be an obvious conclusion." A phrase common to many of the men who were there is that they have been living on borrowed time. Ralph Millsap went on to a very successful career as a public utilities executive. He no doubt speaks for many when he says he has never again had to be so scared. For him, and for many others, facing Death for so long helped build a confidence that contributed to a successful career. Jim Brewer offers perhaps the most fitting ending to the story of that long-ago battle: "Let the dead men rest in their well-earned sleep."[172]

APPENDIX 1

Aleutian Chronology

7 June	Japanese landing forces seize Kiska and Attu.
14 June	General John DeWitt proposes joint operation to expel the Japanese from the Aleutians. Turned down by the War Department.
17 June	Japanese 2nd Submarine Flotilla is deployed to the Aleutians.
18 June	Oiler *Nissan Maru* sunk in Kiska Harbor by fliers of 11th AAF.
3 July	Vice Admiral Hosogaya, the Japanese officer responsible for supplying and maintaining Kiska and Attu, successfully convoys 1,200 men to Kiska.
4 July	The Japanese destroyer *Nenohi* is sunk off Agattu Island by the U.S. submarine *Triton*.
5 July	The destroyer *Arare* is sunk and the destroyers *Kasumi* and *Shiranui* are badly damaged by the U.S. submarine *Growler*.
15 July	Subchasers No. 25 and No. 27 are sunk at Kiska by the U.S. submarine *Grunion*.
30 July	The *Grunion* is lost with all hands; thought to have been mined off Kiska.
7 August	American naval task group under Rear Admiral Smith bombards Kiska; the merchantman *Kano Maru* is damaged.
27 August	Japanese commence evacuating Attu. Troops moved to Kiska.
30 August	U.S. Army forces seize Adak Island to establish airfield. The Japanese submarines RO-61, RO-62, and RO-64 are sent to Adak. The RO-61 manages to torpedo the seaplane tender *Casco* in Nazan Bay, Atka Island. The *Casco* does not sink.
31 August	The RO-61 is sunk by PBYs and the destroyer *Reid*.
16 September	Evacuation of Attu complete. Entire garrison successfully moved to Kiska.

16 October	The destroyer *Oboro* is sunk off Kiska by U.S. B-26 bombers.
26 October	The U.S. submarine *S-31* sinks the *Keizan Maru* off Paramushiro.
30 October	Japanese reoccupy Attu with 1,400 men.
26 November	The merchant ships *Cheribon Maru* and *Kachosan Maru* are sunk at Attu by 11th AAF.
8 December	Admirals King and Nimitz meet in San Francisco. They decide to invade Kiska, but must seek permission from Joint Chiefs.
27 December	The destroyer-minesweeper *Wasmuth* founders and sinks accidentally off the Aleutians.

1943

4 January	Rear Admiral Kinkaid relieves Admiral Theobold as Aleutian theatre commander. Rear Admiral McMorris assumes command of forces afloat.
5 January	11th AAF fliers sink the merchant ships *Montreal Maru* at Kiska and *Kotohiru Maru* at Attu. JCS agree to plan for expulsion of the Japanese from the Aleutians.
12 January	U.S. Army forces seize Amchitka Island to establish another airfield. The destroyer *Worden* is lost through grounding while covering the landing.
14 January	Prime Minister Churchill and President Roosevelt meet at Casablanca. Because of other U.S. commitments, JCS rule out an invasion of Kiska.
5 February	Imperial Navy HQ orders the Aleutians held at all costs.
18 February	A task force under Admiral McMorris bombards Attu. The heavy cruiser *Indianapolis* and two destroyers sink the transport *Akagane Maru* 100 miles SW of Attu.

7 March	Admiral Kinkaid suggests to Washington that Kiska be bypassed and Attu invaded instead.
9 March	A supply convoy from Paramushiro reaches Attu undetected.
11 March	On JCS authority, Admiral Nimitz gives go ahead on plans to invade Attu.
15 March	Acting on communications intelligence, Admiral McMorris departs Dutch Harbor to patrol the sea lanes west of Attu.
22 March	JCS direct operation against Attu to proceed as soon as possible. Admiral Hosogaya leaves Paramushiro with D Convoy, bound for Attu.
26 March	Battle of the Komandorski Islands. Outnumbered nearly two-to-one, Admiral McMorris's task group escapes serious damage after nearly four-hour gunfire duel with Admiral Hosogaya's Fifth Fleet. D Convoy is successfully deterred from reaching Attu.
1 April	Admiral Nimitz and General DeWitt issue final instructions for the invasion of Attu.
15 April	Attu-bound 7th Infantry Division begins to embark at San Francisco.
21 April	Admiral Kinkaid issues op-order covering the invasion of Attu.
26 April	A three-cruiser, six-destroyer task group under Admiral McMorris bombards Attu.
30 April	Attu invasion force arrives in Cold Bay, Alaska.
4 May	Attu invasion force departs Cold Bay for Attu.
11 May	Landings carried out on Attu by first of 11,000-man invasion force.
16 May	Heavy units of the Japanese fleet leave Truk bound for Japan and the Aleutians.
18 May	Admiral McMorris ordered to staff duty in Pearl Harbor.
21 May	Imperial Navy HQ issues instructions for the evacuation of the Aleutians. The operation is to be known as Operation KE-GO.

22 May	Japanese torpedo bombers from Paramushiro attack the American invasion fleet off Attu. Two bombers are shot down.
23 May	Second Japanese air raid on the invasion fleet. American fighters shoot five enemy bombers down, but lose two of their own number.
24 May	JCS authorize planning and training for invasion of Kiska; August 15 set as target date.
26 May	Japanese evacuation of Kiska begins; submarines are used at first.
29 May	Imperial General HQ abandons plans for relief of Attu.
30 May	After a final suicide charge by defenders, Attu is declared secure. Japanese losses are 2,379 dead, 28 POWs; American losses are 600 dead, more than 1,200 wounded.
4 June	JCS approve planned invasion of Kiska.
7 June	Admiral Kinkaid promoted to vice admiral.
21 June	Japanese abandon efforts to evacuate Kiska by submarine. Only 820 personnel have been removed at a cost of three submarines lost to U.S. ASW action.
6 July	A task force under Rear Admiral Giffen bombards Kiska. Rear Admiral Kimura leaves Paramushiro with sixteen ships in an attempt to carry out a surface evacuation of Kiska.
10 July	American Army bombers from Attu raid Paramushiro.
15 July	Japanese evacuation force must return to Paramushiro due to low fuel and insufficient fog cover.
18 July	American Army bombers raid Paramushiro for the second time.
19 July	Admiral Kinkaid gives the final go-ahead for the invasion of Kiska; D-Day is set for 15 August.
22 July	A large American task force bombards Kiska.

	Admiral Kimura leaves Paramushiro for another attempt at evacuation.
26 July	American task group that has bombarded Kiska engages in the "Battle of the Pips." Several hundred rounds are fired at spurious radar contacts.
28 July	Admiral Kimura's evacuation force arrives in Kiska Harbor under cover of heavy fog and successfully carries off 5,183 men.
30 July	Two American destroyers bombard the now-abandoned island of Kiska.
2 August	A large American task force of sixteen warships hurls more than 2,000 rounds into Kiska in a pre-invasion softening up.
10 August– 15 August	11th AAF drops 355 tons of bombs on Kiska. Some pilots report receiving flak, even though there is no one on the island.
12 August	Sixty more tons of naval projectiles are shot into Kiska by a ten-ship task force.
13 August	The invasion force of over 100 ships, carrying 34,000 American and Canadian troops, leaves Adak bound for Kiska.
15 August	Landing made on Kiska; landing force is disbelieving to find the island abandoned. Seventeen American soldiers are killed in fog-bound exchanges of gunfire.
18 August	The destroyer *Abner Read* loses her stern and 70 dead to a drifting Japanese mine off Kiska.
22 August	Kiska declared secure.
August 1943– August 1945	American air and naval forces engage in a series of pinprick raids on Japanese bases in the Kurile Islands. A proposal to base B-29 bombers in the Aleutians is not taken seriously. Except for bases on Adak and at Dutch Harbor, the Aleutians are very quickly abandoned after the Japanese surrender.

Japanese Ship Data

Dimensions and displacement are as designed. Armament is as of March 1943.

NACHI—MYOKO-CLASS HEAVY CRUISER

Displacement: 13,380 (rebuilt)
Dimensions: 668' (oa) × 68' × 20'9" (rebuilt)
Propulsion: 12 Kampon boilers, geared turbines, 4 shafts, 130,000 shp
Speed: 34 knots
Armament: 10 × 8"/50, 8 × 5"/40 DP, 8 × 25-mm AA, 12 × 24" TT, 2 catapults, 2 aircraft
Armor: 4" belt, 2"–3" deck, 6" turrets
Complement: 775
Builder: Kure Navy Yard, 1924–1928
Fate: Sunk in Manila Bay 5 November 1944 by American carrier aircraft.

MAYA—*TAKAO*-CLASS HEAVY CRUISER

Displacement: 13,400 (rebuilt)
Dimensions: 668'6" (oa) × 68' × 20'9" (rebuilt)
Propulsion: 12 Kampon boilers, geared turbines, 4 shafts,
    133,000 shp
Speed: 34 knots
Armament: 10 × 8"/50, 8 × 5"/40 DP, 8 × 25-mm AA, 4
    × 13-mm AA, 16 × 24" TT, 2 catapults, 3 air-
    craft
Armor: 3"–4" belt, 3" deck, 6" turrets
Complement: 775
Builder: Kawasaki, 1928–1932
Fate: Torpedoed and sunk by the USS *Dace* 23 October 1944
    while en route to oppose the Leyte landings.

TAMA—*KUMA*-CLASS LIGHT CRUISER

Displacement: 5,500
Dimensions: 532' (oa) × 46'9" × 15'9"
Propulsion: 12 Kampon boilers, geared turbines, 4 shafts,
    90,000 shp
Speed: 36 knots
Armament: 7 × 5.5"/50, 2 × 3"/40 AA, 8 × 24" TT, 1
    catapult, 1 aircraft
Armor: 2" belt, 1.5"–2" deck
Complement: 439
Builder: Mitsubishi, 1918–1921
Fate: Torpedoed and sunk by the USS *Jallao* 25 October 1944
    NE of Luzon.

ABUKUMA—*NAGARA*-CLASS LIGHT CRUISER

Displacement: 5,170
Dimensions: 534'9" (oa) × 48'5" × 16'
Propulsion: 12 Kampon boilers, geared turbines, 4 shafts,
    90,000 shp
Speed: 36 knots
Armament: 7 × 5.5"/50, 2 × 3"/40 AA, 8 × 24" TT

Armor: 2″ belt, 1.5″–2″ deck
Complement: 440
Builder: Uraga, 1921–1925
Fate: Sunk by U.S. Army B-24 bombers 26 October 1944 in
     Leyte Gulf.

INAZUMA, IKAZUCHI—AKATSUKI-CLASS DESTROYERS

Displacement: 1,680
Dimensions: 371′6″ (oa) × 34′ × 10′9″
Propulsion: 3 Kampon boilers, geared turbines, 2 shafts, 50,000
          shp
Speed: 38 knots
Armament: 6 × 5″/50 DP, 2 × 13-mm AA, 9 × 24″ TT
Complement: 250
Builder: *Inazuma*—Fujinagata, 1930–1932
     Ikazuchi—Uraga, 1930–1932
Fate: *Inazuma* torpedoed and sunk by the USS *Bonefish* 14
     May 1944 off Tawi Tawi.
     Ikazuchi torpedoed and sunk by the USS *Harder* 13 April
     1944 200 miles SSE Guam.

HATSUSHIMO, WAKABA—HATSUHARA-CLASS
DESTROYERS

Displacement: 1,715
Dimensions: 359′3″ (oa) × 32′9″ × 9′11″
Propulsion: 3 Kampon boilers, geared turbines, 2 shafts, 42,000
          shp
Speed: 33 knots
Armament: 5 × 5″/50 DP, 2 × 13-mm AA, 9 × 24″ TT
Complement: 230
Builder: *Hatsushimo*, Uraga, 1933–1934
     Wakaba, Sasebo Navy Yard, 1931–1934
Fate: *Hatsushimo* mined 30 July 1945 WNW Maizuru.
     Wakaba sunk by carrier aircraft 24 October 1944 off
     Panay.

APPENDIX 3

American Ship Data

Dimensions and displacement are as designed. Armament is as of March 1943.

SALT LAKE CITY—*PENSACOLA*-CLASS HEAVY CRUISER

Displacement: 9,100
Dimensions: 585′6″ (oa) × 65′3″ × 22′
Propulsion: 8 White-Foster boilers, geared turbines, 4 shafts, 107,000 shp
Speed: 32 knots.
Armament: 10 × 8″/55, 8 × 5″/25 DP, 24 × 40-mm AA, 19 × 20-mm AA, 2 catapults, 2 aircraft
Armor: 3″ belt, 2″–1″ deck, 1.5″ turrets
Complement: 1,200 plus
Builder: New York Shipbuilding Co., 1927–1929
Fate: Used as target; sunk 25 May 1948 off coast of California.

RICHMOND—*OMAHA*-CLASS LIGHT CRUISER

Displacement: 7,400
Dimensions: 555′6″ (oa) × 55′4″ × 20′
Propulsion: 12 Yarrow boilers, geared turbines, 4 shafts, 90,000 shp

Speed: 35 knots
Armament: 10 × 6″/53, 8 × 3″/50 AA, 4 × 40-mm AA, 6 × 21″ TT, 2 catapults, 2 aircraft
Armor: 3″ belt, 1.5″ deck
Complement: 823
Builder: William Cramp, 1920–1923
Fate: Decommissioned 12 December 1945; broken up 1946.

DALE, MONAGHAN—FARRAGUT-CLASS DESTROYERS

Displacement: 1,500
Dimensions: 341′3″ (oa) × 34′3″ × 15.5
Propulsion: 4 Yarrow boilers, geared turbines, 2 shafts, 42,800 shp
Speed: 36.5 knots
Armament: 4 × 5″/38 DP, 4 × 40-mm AA, 5 × 20-mm AA, 8 × 21″ TT
Complement: 260
Builder: *Dale*, NY Navy Yard, 1934–1935
Monaghan, Boston Navy Yard, 1933–1935
Fate: *Dale* decommissioned 6 October 1945, sold 20 December 1946.
Monaghan foundered 18 December 1944 while caught in typhoon near the Philippine Islands.

BAILEY, COGHLAN—BENSON-CLASS DESTROYERS

Displacement: 1,620
Dimensions: 348′4″ (oa) × 36′1″ × 19′8″
Propulsion: 4 Babcock and Wilcox boilers, geared turbines, 2 shafts, 50,000 shp
Speed: 37 knots
Armament: 4 × 5″/38 DP, 4 × 40-mm AA, 5 × 20-mm AA, 5 × 21″ TT
Complement: 260
Builder: *Bailey*, Bethlehem NY, 1941–1942
Coghlan, Bethlehem SF, 1941–1942
Fate: *Bailey* decommissioned 2 May 1946; stricken 1 May 1968.
Coghlan decommissioned 31 March 1947; stricken 1 July 1971.

APPENDIX 4

Gunnery and Torpedo Data

AMMUNITION EXPENDED BY TG 16.6

Ship	8"	6"	5"	3"	Torpedoes
Salt Lake City	806 AP 26 HC		102		
Richmond		271		24	
Bailey			482		5 × 21"
Coghlan			750		
Monaghan			235		
Dale			728		

AMMUNITION EXPENDED BY FIFTH FLEET

Ship	8"	5.5"	5.1"	Torpedoes
Nachi	707		276	16 × 24"
Maya	904		9	8 × 24"
Abukuma		95		4 × 24"
Tama		45(?)		4 × 24"
Wakaba			Unknown	6 × 24"
Hatsushimo			Unknown	4 × 24"

There is no data available for the other two Japanese destroyers.

CONTROL

Visual means of control were paramount in this battle. All the American ships were equipped with search and fire-control radars. The latter proved to be susceptible to gunfire shock and were generally ineffective at the long ranges that prevailed. The newer SG search radar carried by all but the *Bailey* and the *Coghlan* was reliable and accurate.

None of the Japanese ships carried radar, but the control of the heavy cruisers was excellent. Despite the smoke screen, both the *Nachi* and the *Maya* brought quick and accurate fire to bear whenever the *Salt Lake City* came into view. Over 200 blue-dyed shell splashes were counted within fifty yards of the *Salt Lake City*. Japanese salvo patterns remained uniformly tight; Captain Rodgers reported the average Japanese shell pattern to be about 250 to 300 yards in range and thirty yards in deflection. He felt more hits would have been scored had the dispersion been greater.

MISCELLANEOUS GUNNERY NOTES

The *Salt Lake City* suffered a bore constriction in the left gun of Turret I of .002″ and in the left gun of Turret IV of .006″–.011″. Japanese shell splashes were observed to be blue, green, yellow, and occasionally maroon. They were also smaller than the American splashes, as most of the Japanese shells detonated well below the water's surface, if at all. The *Salt Lake City* fired 66 percent of her 8-inch ammunition.

The accounts of Commanders Miura and Hashimoto indicate that the majority of the *Salt Lake City*'s shells fell close aboard the *Nachi*, with the preponderance of misses falling ahead. Commander Hashimoto felt more hits would have been scored on the Japanese ship had the *Salt Lake City*'s dispersion been greater. He also stated that both Japanese heavy cruisers carried 1,100 rounds of 8-inch ammunition; the *Maya* therefore fired approximately 82 percent of hers and the *Nachi* 64 percent of hers.

TORPEDO DATA

The effectiveness of Japanese torpedoes has often been covered in other histories, but the awesome nature of those weapons is still worth noting. The standard shipboard weapon of the Imperial Navy was the Type 93 Model 1, oxygen-fueled torpedo. It weighed over 6,000 pounds, had a 1,200-pound warhead, and a range of 22,000 yards at 49 knots, or 44,000 yards at 36 knots. In contrast, American torpedoes weighed 3,841 pounds, had warheads of 825 pounds, and a slow-speed, maximum range of 15,000 yards. The effectiveness of Japanese torpedoes was enhanced by the refusal of the United States Navy to believe that its ships were being torpedoed at such extreme ranges.

Damage and Casualties to TG 16.6

The following are listings of damage and casualties not covered in the narrative.

Salt Lake City: Five bow compartments flooded or partially flooded as a result of the hit in the chain locker. As a result of the after 5-inch magazine being flooded, 1,032 rounds of 5-inch Common and 260 rounds of 5-inch Illumination ammunition were lost. The hit amidships damaged the catapult and the forward Mk 4 fire-control radar, punctured the stacks and searchlight platform, and badly gouged the barrel of Number III 5-inch gun. Gun blast from the after turrets badly damaged the after 40-mm director, the mounts and gun shields. Blast damage caused 712 rounds of 40-mm ammunition to be jettisoned. In addition to the two men killed, shrapnel wounded twenty-seven others.

Bailey: Forward main turbine and reduction gear bearings seized due to failure of lube-oil pump. Five dead and three seriously wounded.

Coghlan: Three shrapnel holes in the main battery director, several in the stacks and bridge area. The Mk 4 fire-control radar was disabled, the radar transmitter smashed, and the whaleboat holed.

Monaghan: No battle damage, but Number IV boiler seriously damaged due to the necessity of going from cold iron to full power at the outset of the action. No personnel casualties.

The other two ships of the task group received no damage.

The Battle Refought

After all the pertinent Action Reports were in, the Battle of the Komandorski Islands was refought on the game board at the U.S. Naval War College. Not surprisingly, the results were somewhat different from the actual battle.

REFIGHTING THE BATTLE

After considering the tactical dispositions, the following material factors were weighed:

The *Salt Lake City* was considered to be the equal in speed and fire power to either of the Japanese heavy cruisers. Of course, she was outnumbered. The Japanese cruisers were considered able to out-range SLC, but the actual ranges at which the battle was fought made the consideration immaterial.

The *Richmond* was considered to be superior to either of the Japanese light cruisers, but again, she was also outnumbered. Her main battery out-ranged that of the Japanese light cruisers.

The American destroyers were considered to be the equal in speed and durability to the Japanese destroyers. The Japanese destroyers were considered able to out-range the American destroyers by 1,000 yards.

The performance of Japanese torpedoes was again grossly underestimated, as they were allowed only a 15,000 yard range.

ASSESSING DAMAGE

The following theoretical damage curves were used:

Against the *Salt Lake City*, the *Nachi* and the *Maya* were considered able to get (a) side penetration with a target angle of 90° at and below 18,000 yards; (b) side penetration with a target angle of 45° at and below 10,000 yards; (c) deck penetration at and above 23,000 yards. Against the *Richmond*, they were considered able to get (a) side penetration with a target angle of 90° at and below 31,000 yards; (b) side penetration with a 45° target angle at and below 22,000 yards.

Against the *Salt Lake City*, the *Abukuma* and the *Tama* were considered able to get (a) side penetration with a 90° target angle at and below 14,000 yards; (b) side penetration with a 45° target angle at and below 8,000 yards; (c) deck penetration at and above 16,000 yards.

Against the *Salt Lake City*, the Japanese destroyers were considered able to get (a) side penetration with a 90° target angle at and below 10,000 yards; (b) side penetration with a 45° target angle at and below 5,000 yards. Against the *Richmond*, they were considered able to get (a) side penetration with a 90° target angle at and below 10,000 yards; (b) side penetration with a 45° target angle at and below 6,000 yards.

Against the Japanese heavy cruisers, the *Salt Lake City* was considered able to get (a) side penetration with a 90° target angle at and below 23,000 yards; (b) side penetration with a 45° target angle at and below 13,000 yards; (c) deck penetration at and above 23,000 yards.

Against the Japanese heavy cruisers, the *Richmond* was considered able to get (a) side penetration with a 90° target angle at and below 6,000 yards; (b) no side penetration with a 45° target angle; (c) no deck penetration. Against the Japanese light cruisers, the *Richmond* was considered able to get (a) side penetration with a 90° target angle at and below 13,000 yards; (b) side penetration with a target angle of 45° at and below 9,000 yards; (c) side penetration with a target angle of 45° at and below 9,000 yards; (c) deck penetration at and above 18,000 yards.

Against the Japanese heavy cruisers, the American destroyers were considered able to get (a) side penetration with a 90° target angle at and below 1,000 yards; (b) no side penetration with a 45° target angle. Against the Japanese light cruisers, they were considered able to get (a) side penetration with a 90° target angle at and below 7,000 yards; (b) side penetration with a 45° target angle at and below 4,000 yards.

PENALTIES

The *Salt Lake City* was penalized for not launching a spotter, and the value of her radar as a fire-control instrument was negated by the inexperience of her control personnel. The Japanese heavy cruisers were awarded an advantage for having an air spotter.

RESULTS

The theoretical battle ended after fifty-one moves. As illustrated by the account on page 159 in the narrative, the theoretical outcome was far different from the real outcome.

Notes

Several abbreviations appear in these notes: *Salt Lake City* (SLC); letter (ltr); Action Report (AR); Rear Admiral McMorris (CTG 16.6); United States Strategic Bombing Survey (USSBS). Material derived from an interview is so indicated the first time cited, thereafter only an individual's name appears.

1. "The World Turned Upside Down" was the particularly appropriate tune played by the British military band as Lord Cornwallis surrendered to Washington at Yorktown.

2. Winterbotham, Fred W., *The Ultra Secret*.

3. Morison, Samuel E., *The Two-Ocean War*, p. 9.

4. Technical information and ship's histories are drawn from Jentschura, Hansgeorg, *Warships of the Imperial Japanese Navy*; Watts, Anthony, *Japanese Warships in World War II*; Dull, Paul S., *A Battle History of the Imperial Japanese Navy*, pp. 49–259. See also Holmes, W. J., *Double Edged Secrets*, pp. 132–133, for information concerning the *Maya*'s unexpected presence in North Pacific waters.

5. See Appendix Four.

6. Marder, Arthur, "Bravery is Not Enough," p. 10.

7. O'Connell, George, personal account of the battle.

8. Ibid.

9. SLC Memorandum of 17 March 1943; Grahn, tape.

10. *The War Cruises of USS Salt Lake City*, pp. 6–8.

11. The SLC was often referred to in the popular press as the "Swayback Maru." Among some of her crew, she was also known as the "Shitsey Maru." Mores of the 1940s allowed only the former name to appear in print. Dahlen, interview 8/18/81; Michael, ltr.

12. Naval Historical Center biography of V Adm B. J. Rodgers, 11/1/71; Bitler, interview 7/8/81; Brewer, interview 7/15/81; Johnston, interview 5/30/81; Dahlen.

13. Rodgers, interview 8/17/81; Bitler.

14. Hodge, interview 6/25/81; Johnston.

15. Engle, ltr 10/27/81; Morison, Samuel E., *History of US Naval Operations in World War II*, vol. 7, p. 23; Brewer; Johnston.

16. Brewer, ltr 10/25/81.

17. Taplett, ltr.

18. Brewer.

19. Harrison, tape; Millsap, interview 6/10/81.

20. Ales, ltr 7/1/81.

21. Turner, ltr.

22. Miller, tape.

23. Purdy, ltr; Branneman, ltr 9/9/81; Millsap; Miller, tape.

24. Miller, Jerry, U.S. Naval Institute Oral History interview transcript, pp. 77–78.

25. Purdy, ltr.

26. Miller, Oral History, pp. 68–69.

27. Kait, ltr 9/20/81.

28. Graffius, ltr 7/7/81; Wiest, ltr 9/21/81; Luscher, ltr.

29. Brown, ltr.

30. Robinson, interview 7/16/81; Walker, ltr 8/14/81.

31. Kait, ltr; Ovrum, interview 8/18/81; Robinson,.

32. Ayers, ltr 9/25/81.

33. Bumpus, tape.

34. Walker, ltr 8/5/81.

35. Ayers, ltr.

36. Bumpas, tape.

37. Peckham, ltr 10/9/81.

38. Atkeson, interview 7/6/81.

39. James, ltr 10/8/81.

40. Brewer; Vasey, interview 5/31/81.

41. Millsap.

42. Ovrum.

43. Harrison, tape.

44. O'Connell, personal account.

45. Johnston.

46. Brown, ltr.

47. Millsap; Branneman, ltr.; Atkeson; Bumpas, tape.

48. Taplett, ltr.

49. SLC Deck Log 3/26/43; AR USS *Monaghan* 3/29/43, p. 2; Morison, *Two-Ocean War*, p. 26.

50. AR CTG 16.6 4/6/43, p. 7; AR USS SLC 4/1/43, p. 2.

51. Millsap; Bitler; Grahn, tape; Johnston; Vasey; Jenkins, ltr 8/6/81.

52. O'Connell, personal account.

53. James, ltr, Grahn, tape, Bitler; Miller, tape.

54. AR CTG 16.6, p. 7.

55. Millsap; Miller, tape.

56. USSBS, *Interrogations of Japanese Officials*, vol. I, p. 99. The Japanese officer being interrogated testified that the *Nachi* and both Pete and Jake aircraft embarked. Another Japanese officer said that none of the other cruisers had aircraft embarked. Dull, p. 264, states that according to the *Maya*'s AR, gun blasts set her No. 1 plane ablaze.

57. Branneman, ltr.

58. Millsap; Turner, ltr.

59. O'Connell, personal account.

60. Turner, ltr.

61. Johnston.

62. Millsap.

63. O'Connell, personal account.

64. AR CTG 16.6, p. 9.

65. Brewer; Johnston; Bitler; Matusek, ltr 8/26/81; AR USS *Coghlan* 3/27/43, p. 2; AR USS *Monaghan*, p. 1.

66. Millsap; Miller, tape.

67. USSBS, vol. I, pp. 99 and 112; the validity of these interrogations has been decried in certain quarters. While they do have faults, the accuracy of the information provided by each interrogated officer is assessed at the end of vol. II. In the case of Commander Miura, it is stated that "He spoke freely but tended to minimize the

damage to both Japanese and U.S. Forces" (p. 559). In the case of Commander Hashimoto, it is stated that "He was intelligent and cooperative, and his information was generally quite accurate" (p. 550).

68. Johnston; Robinson; Naval War College Study of the Battle of the Komandorski Islands, 6/8/43, p. 5.

69. Japanese Monograph #89, "Northern Area Naval Operations," Annexed Table No. 1.

70. AR CTG 16.6, p. 10; AR USS *Richmond* 3/28/43, p. 2; Bitler; Millsap; AR USS *Bailey* 3/28/43, p. 6; Purdy, ltr.

71. Miller, tape.

72. Brewer.

73. Mihalka, ltr 6/9/81; Woolworth, ltr 6/23/81; Brewer; Harrison, tape; Harrison, tape; Bitler.

74. Bitler.

75. There is a divergence of opinion among SLC men on this subject. Her AR seems to indicate that the radars were of limited usefulness in directing gunfire though perfectly adequate in tracking the enemy's movements. The radarmen felt the radar was satisfactory, while the gunners maintain they depended on what they could see. Brewer; Lee, ltr; Johnston; O'Connell, personal account; Ramsey, ltr 11/30/81; AR USS SLC, p. 29.

76. Robinson.

77. Abrams, ltr.

78. Morison, vol. 7, p. 27; AR CTG 16.6, p. 13; AR navigator, USS *Richmond*, p. 3.

79. AR CTG 16.6, p. 11.

80. Reeves, ltr.

81. Ibid.

82. Johnston.

83. Ibid.

84. Johnston; Callahan, ltr 4/8/81.

85. Grahn, tape.

86. O'Hara, ltr 3/21/81; Bacues, ltr; Robinson.

87. Rodgers; Bitler.

88. Brewer; Grahn, tape; Engle, ltr; O'Connell, personal account.

89. Bitler; Vasey; Hodge.

90. Walker, ltr.

91. Ayers, ltr.
92. Ales, ltr.
93. Duren, ltr.
94. Bacues, ltr; Engebrecht, ltr 9/20/81; Graffius, ltr.
95. Reeves, ltr.
96. Grahn, tape.
97. O'Connell, personal account.
98. Engle, ltr.
99. AR CTG 16.6, p. 20.
100. Rodebaugh, ltr 10/4/81.
101. O'Connell, personal account.
102. Miller, tape.
103. O'Connell, personal account.
104. AR USS *Monaghan*, p. 3; Bangert, ltr 8/23/81.
105. O'Connell, personal account.
106. Lanman, ltr.
107. Ibid.
108. Bitler; Matison, ltr; McCarthy, ltr 10/25/81.
109. Kleinschmit, ltr 9/18/81; Mihalka, ltr; Bacues, ltr; Van Kessel, ltr. 10/3/81.
110. Dahlen; Mew, ltr. Dull says the *Abukuma* scored this hit, but fragments recovered at Mare Island show it was an 8-inch shell. Dull, *A Battle History*, p. 264.
111. Dahlen; Dahlen, ltr 9/3/81; AR USS SLC, p. 18.
112. Dahlen.
113. O'Connell, personal account.
114. Duren, ltr.
115. Robinson.
116. USSBS, vol. II, p. 402.
117. Matusek, ltr.
118. Engle, ltr.
119. O'Connell, ltr 9/20/81; Morison, vol. 7, p. 32.
120. Brewer; Johnston; O'Connell, personal account; Bitler; Matusek, ltr.
121. Dahlen.
122. Dahlen; Johnston; Brewer.
123. Millsap; Robinson; Norwood, ltr 10/7/81; Callahan, ltr.
124. Bitler; Brewer; Hosey, interview 6/21/81; Webb, ltr; Johnston.

125. Matusek, ltr; Taplett, ltr; Yates, ltr; Reeves, ltr.

126. O'Connell, personal account.

127. Drust, ltr 10/18/81; Bennett, ltr 9/24/81; Brewer.

128. Dahlen; Johnston, ltr.

129. Peckham, ltr; Millsap.

130. Stahlberg, ltr.

131. James, ltr.

132. USSBS, vol. I, p. 99.

133. Bitler; Purdy, ltr; Johnston.

134. Ayers, ltr.

135. Ayers, ibid.; Walker, ltr.

136. Kait, ltr; Atkeson.

137. USSBS, vol. I, p. 100.

138. Roscoe, Theodore, *United States Destroyer Operations in World War II*, p. 161.

139. Bumpas, tape.

140. James, ltr; AR USS Bailey, p. 4; USSBS, vol. II, p. 305.

141. James, ltr.

142. Ibid.

143. Branneman, ltr 9/8/81; Robinson; Hoke, ltr 9/15/79.

144. Atkeson; Millsap; Ovrum.

145. Hodge; Brewer; Vasey; Matusek, ltr; Melville, ltr 3/31/81.

146. Millsap; USSBS, vol. II, pp. 305 and 400.

147. Addition to AR USS SLC of 4/8/43, p. 2; Grahn, tape.

148. Robinson; Callahan, ltr.

149. Moreau, ltr 10/22/81; Putrelo, ltr.

150. Ales, ltr; Robinson.

151. Graffius, ltr; Bitler.

152. Johnston.

153. Mew, ltr.

154. Morison attributes this entry to an Ensign Lloyd, but an examination of the handwriting in the SLC's Deck Log leaves no doubt that the entry was made by Hawkins. USS SLC Deck Log, 3/26/43; Morison, vol. 7, p. 36.

155. O'Hara, ltr; Reeves, ltr.

156. Drust, ltr.

157. Atkeson.

158. Rodebaugh, ltr; Hodge.

159. James, ltr.
160. Brown, ltr; Vasey; Johnston; Bumpas, tape.
161. Ayers, ltr; O'Hara, ltr.
162. Bennett, ltr.
163. Miller, tape.
164. Ibid.
165. Johnston; Bitler, ltr 6/12/81; Brewer; Robinson.
166. AR CTG 16.6, p. 24.
167. Miller, tape; Brewer.
168. Rodgers; Callahan, ltr; James, ltr.
169. Naval War College Study, p. 71; AR USS SLC, p. 49.
170. USSBS, vol. I, pp. 99 and 112; Miura says 40 personnel were killed, while Hashimoto mentions only the men killed when the *Nachi* was first hit. USSBS, vol. II, p. 401; the historical record states the *Nachi* suffered 15 killed and 27 wounded.
171. Dahlen.
172. Graffius, ltr; Millsap; Brewer.

Sources

INTERVIEWS AND CORRESPONDENCE

Name	Rate/Rank 3/26/43	Ship
Abrams, Charles	Radioman 3c	*Dale*
Ales, George, CDR USN (Ret.)	Electrician's Mate 1c	*Richmond*
Amdahl, Raymond	Gunner's Mate 1c	*Salt Lake City*
Andrews, Frank	Signalman 1c	*Monaghan*
Atkeson, John RADM, USN (Ret.)	Lieutenant Commander	*Bailey*
Ayers, Frank, CDR, USN (Ret.)	Lieutenant (jg)	*Bailey*
Bacues, Jack	Seaman 1c	*Salt Lake City*
Bangert, Earl ETC, USN (Ret.)	Storekeeper 3c	*Monaghan*
Bennett, Lacy	Gunner's Mate 3c	*Salt Lake City*
Berry, A. D., ACCM, USN (Ret.)		*Richmond*

197

SOURCES

Name	Rate/Rank 3/26/43	Ship
Bitler, W. S., RADM, USN (Ret.)	Commander	*Salt Lake City*
Bixler, Clifford, CWO, USN (Ret.)	Chief Shipfitter	*Richmond*
Branneman, Leonard, CAPT, USN (Ret.)	Lieutenant Commander	*Richmond*
Brewer, Jim, RADM, USN (Ret.)	Lieutenant Commander	*Salt Lake City*
Brown, Ed	Seaman 1c	*Monaghan*
Bryant, Lehman, BTC, USN (Ret.)	Chief Watertender	*Richmond*
Callahan, Mike	Lieutenant	*Dale*
Campbell, Cliff		*Monaghan*
Carroll, C. H., CAPT, USN (Ret.)		*Salt Lake City*
Dahlen, Vince, CDR, USN (Ret.)	Ensign	*Salt Lake City*
Drust, Roy, YNC, USN (Ret.)	Yeoman 1c	*Salt Lake City*
Duren, Elmer	Watertender 2c	*Dale*
Engebrecht, Elmer, HTC, USN (Ret.)	Shipfitter 1c	*Salt Lake City*
Engle, Jerry, CAPT, USN (Ret.)	Lieutenant	*Salt Lake City*
Erickson, Clayton	Torpedoman 3c	*Monaghan*
Gaviglio, Peter, CAPT, USN (Ret.)	Lieutenant Commander	*Richmond*
Graffius, Dick	Firecontrolman 1c	*Monaghan*
Grahn, Howard, CAPT, USNR (Ret.)	Lieutenant	*Salt Lake City*
Harrison, Chuck, LCDR, USNR (Ret.)	Lieutenant	*Richmond*
Hodge, Rev. Father Richard, CDR, USNR (Ret.)	Lieutenant (Chaplain)	*Salt Lake City*
Hoke, Herman, DCC, USN (Ret.)	Carpenter's Mate	*Dale*
Holcomb, James		*Richmond*

198

SOURCES

Name	Rate/Rank 3/26/43	Ship
Hosey, Bill, CDR, USN (Ret.)	Lieutenant (jg)	*Salt Lake City*
James, John, CDR, USN (Ret.)	Lieutenant (jg)	*Coghlan*
Jenkins, Walter, CAPT, USN (Ret.)	Lieutenant Commander	Staff—Adak
Johnston, Ben, CAPT, USN (Ret.)	Lieutenant	*Salt Lake City*
Kait, Hart, CAPT, USN (Ret.)	Lieutenant Commander	*Monaghan*
Kleinschmit, Paul	Seaman 2c	*Salt Lake City*
Lanman, Jim, AKC, USN (Ret.)*	Storekeeper 2c	*Salt Lake City*
Lee, Chet, CAPT, USN (Ret.)	Lieutenant (jg)	*Salt Lake City*
Lewis, Ed, LCDR, USN (Ret.)	Gunner's Mate 2c	*Salt Lake City*
London, Bill, CWO, USN (Ret.)	Electrician's Mate 1c	*Monaghan*
Luscher, Al	Seaman 1c	*Monaghan*
Matison, Carl, EMC, USN (Ret.)	Electrician's Mate 1c	*Salt Lake City*
Matusek, Bob, CDR, USNR (Ret.)	Lieutenant	*Salt Lake City*
McCarthy, Dick	Machinist's Mate 1c	*Salt Lake City*
Melville, Al	Seaman 1c	*Salt Lake City*
Mew, Jim, CDR, USN (Ret.)	Ensign	*Salt Lake City*
Michael, Cyrus	Fireman 1c	*Salt Lake City*
Mihalka, Alex, BMCM, USNR (Ret.)	Bosun's Mate 1c	*Salt Lake City*
Miller, Jerry, VADM, USN (Ret.)	Lieutenant (jg)	*Richmond*
Millsap, Ralph, CDR, USNR (Ret.)	Lieutenant	*Richmond*
Moore, Frank, CWO, USN (Ret.)	Chief Warrant Officer	*Salt Lake City*

Name	Rate/Rank 3/26/43	Ship
Moureau, Ralph, CAPT, USN (Ret.)	Lieutenant	Bailey
Nickerson, Arthur	Gunner's Mate 2c	Salt Lake City
Norwood, Larry	Seaman 2c	Dale
O'Connell, George, CAPT, USN (Ret.)	Lieutenant	Salt Lake City
O'Hara, Jim	Seaman 1c	Salt Lake City
Ovrum, Al, CAPT, USN (Ret.)	Lieutenant Commander	Richmond
Peckham, George, RADM, USN (Ret.)	Lieutenant Commander	DesRon 14— Bailey
Purdy, Gene, YNC, USN (Ret.)	Yeoman 2c	Richmond
Putrelo, Carmine	Fireman 2c	Bailey
Ramsey, Lyle, CAPT, USN (Ret.)	Lieutenant	Salt Lake City
Riley, C. W.	Machinist's Mate 1c	Monaghan
Robinson, Ken, CAPT, USN (Ret.)	Lieutenant Commander	Dale
Rodebaugh, Jerry	Seaman 1c	Salt Lake City
Rodgers, Bertram, VADM, USN (Ret.)*	Captain	Salt Lake City
Reeves, Gerry, CAPT, USN (Ret.)	Lieutenant (jg)	Salt Lake City
Stahlberg, Ernest	Machinist's Mate 1c	Monaghan
Taplett, Bob, COL, USMC (Ret.)	Major	Salt Lake City
Thomas, Gid	Mess Attendant 3c	Richmond
Turner, James	Coxswain	Richmond
Van Kessel, Mike	Seaman 2c	Salt Lake City
Vasey, Chuck, CDR (SC), USN (Ret.)	Yeoman 1c	Salt Lake City
Walker, Billy, BTC, USN (Ret.)	Fireman 1c	Dale

SOURCES

Name	Rate/Rank 3/26/43	Ship
Walker, Bob	Gunner's Mate 3c	*Bailey*
Webb, Lloyd	Seaman 1c	*Salt Lake City*
Wells, Warren	Bosun's Mate 1c	*Salt Lake City*
Wiest, Dan	Pharmacist's Mate 2c	*Monaghan*
Williams, Don		*Salt Lake City*
Wright, John, ABHC, USN (Ret.)		*Richmond*
Woolworth, Rod	Seaman 1c	*Salt Lake City*
Yates, Roy	Watertender 2c	*Salt Lake City*

* Deceased

RECORDS AND REPORTS

Action Report, Commander Task Group 16.6, 6 April 1943
Action Report, Commander Destroyer Squadron 14, 27 March 1943
Action Report, USS *Bailey*, 28 March 1943
Action Report, USS *Coghlan*, 27 March 1943
Action Report, USS *Monaghan*, 29 March 1943
Action Report, USS *Richmond*, 28 March 1943
Action Report, USS *Salt Lake City*, 1 April 1943
Buships War Damage Report Number 42, USS *Salt Lake City*, 28 July 1943
Combat Narratives: The Aleutians Campaign June 1942–August 1943; "The Battle of the Komandorski Islands", pp. 27–64.
Japanese Monograph Number 89; "Northern Area Naval Operations, February 1942–August 1945."
Naval War College Study of the Battle of the Komandorski Islands, 8 June 1943
USSBS (Pacific), Naval Analysis Division, Interrogations of Japanese Officials, Vols I and II; "Transports at the Battle of the Komandorski Islands; 26 March 1943"; "Operations of Japanese First Destroyer Squadron"; "Japanese Historical Account of the Battle of the Komandorski Islands"; Washington, U.S. Government Printing Office, 1946.
War Diary, USS *Richmond*, 1–31 March 1943
War Diary, USS *Salt Lake City*, 1–31 March 1943

Bibliography

BOOKS

Anonymous, *The War Cruises of the USS Salt Lake City*. USS *Salt Lake City*, 1946.

Craven, Wesley F. and James L. Cate. *The Army Air Forces in World War II: Guadalcanal to Saipan*. Chicago: Chicago University Press, 1950.

Dull, Paul S. *A Battle History of the Imperial Japanese Navy*. Annapolis: Naval Institute Press, 1978.

Fahey, James. *The Ships and Aircraft of the U.S. Fleet: Victory Edition*. Annapolis: Naval Institute Press, 1976.

Fitzsimons, Bernard, ed. *Encyclopedia of 20th Century Weapons and Warfare*, vol. 16. New York: Columbia House, 1978.

Friedman, Norman. *U.S. Destroyers: An Illustrated Design History*. Annapolis: Naval Institute Press, 1982.

———. *U.S. Naval Weapons*. Annapolis: Naval Institute Press, 1982.

Garfield, Brian. *The Thousand Mile War: World War II in the Aleutians*. New York: Ballantine Books, 1969.

Holmes, W. J. *Double Edged Secrets: U.S. Naval Intelligence Operations in the Pacific During World War II*. Annapolis: Naval Institute Press, 1979.

BIBLIOGRAPHY

Hoyt, Edwin P. *How They Won the War in the Pacific: Nimitz and His Admirals.* New York: Weybright and Talley, 1970.

Jentschura, Hansgeorg, et al. *Warships of the Imperial Japanese Navy: 1869–1945.* Annapolis: Naval Institute Press, 1977.

Morison, Samuel Eliot. *History of United States Naval Operations in World War II*; vols. II and VII. Boston: Little, Brown & Co., 1951.

————. *The Two-Ocean War.* Boston: Little, Brown & Co., 1963.

Parrish, Thomas, ed. *The Simon Schuster Encyclopedia of World War II.* New York: Simon Schuster, 1978.

Rigge, Simon. *War in the Outposts.* Alexandria: Time-Life Books, 1980.

Rowher, Jurgen and G. Hummelchen. *Chronology of the War at Sea: 1939–1945*; vols. I and II. London: Ian Allan, 1972–74.

Roscoe, Theodore. *United States Destroyer Operations In World War II.* Annapolis: U.S. Naval Institute, 1953.

Silverstone, Paul H. *U.S. Warships in World War II.* New York: Doubleday and Co., 1962.

Watts, Anthony J. *Japanese Warships in World War II.* London: Ian Allan, 1967.

Winterbotham, Fred W. *The Ultra Secret.* New York: Harper & Row, 1974.

PERIODICALS

Anonymous. "Elegy for Old Swayback." *The Milwaukee Journal,* 17 May 1948.

Anonymous. "Fighting Ship's Ghost Walks." Paper unknown; datelined Salt Lake City, Utah, 26 May 1948.

Anonymous. "Navy Ships, Planes Sink Cruiser Salt Lake City." Paper unknown; datelined, With the United States First Task Fleet, 26 May 1948.

Anonymous. "Tell Story of Aleutian Sea Battle." *The San Francisco News.*

Bishop, John. "My Speed Zero." *The Saturday Evening Post,* 5 February 1944.

Friedman, Norman. "The Salt Lake City Class." *Warship,* 1978.

Marder, Arthur. "Bravery is Not Enough: The Rise and Fall of the Imperial Japanese Navy (1941–1945)." U.C. Irvine, 7 February 1978.

BIBLIOGRAPHY

Pratt, Fletcher. "They Called Her Swayback Maru." *Saga Magazine*, June 1956.

Worden, William. "How 6 U.S. Ships Rout 12 Japs in Arctic Battle." *The Chicago Tribune*, 5 May 1943.

Wright, Christopher. "Comparative Notes on U.S. Treaty Cruiser Design." *Warship International*, no. 4, 1980.

Index

207

INDEX